THE WHITE HOUSE

WASHINGTON

August 9, 1974

Dear Mr. Secretary:

I hereby resign the Office of President of the
United States.

Sincerely,

Richard Nixon

11.35 AM

The Honorable Henry A. Kissinger
The Secretary of State
Washington, D.C. 20520

HK

THE FALL OF RICHARD NIXON

A Reporter
Remembers Watergate

RANDOM HOUSE
NEW YORK

THE FALL OF
RICHARD NIXON

TOM BROKAW

Copyright © 2019 by Tom Brokaw

All rights reserved.

Published in the United States by Random House, an imprint
and division of Penguin Random House LLC, New York.

RANDOM HOUSE and the HOUSE colophon are
registered trademarks of Penguin Random House LLC.

LIBRARY OF CONGRESS CATALOGING-IN-PUBLICATION DATA
NAMES: Brokaw, Tom, author.
TITLE: The fall of Richard Nixon: a reporter remembers Watergate / Tom Brokaw.
DESCRIPTION: First edition. | New York: Random House, [2019] | Includes index.
IDENTIFIERS: LCCN 2019029798 (print) | LCCN 2019029799 (ebook) |
ISBN 9781400069705 (hardcover) | ISBN 9780679604679 (ebook)
SUBJECTS: LCSH: Nixon, Richard M. (Richard Milhous), 1913-1994. |
Watergate Affair, 1972-1974—Press coverage. |
United States—Politics and government—1969-1974.
CLASSIFICATION: LCC E860 .B76 2019 (print) | LCC E860 (ebook) |
DDC 973.924092 [B]—dc23
LC record available at lccn.loc.gov/2019029798
LC ebook record available at lccn.loc.gov/2019029799

Printed in the United States of America on acid-free paper

randomhousebooks.com

2 4 6 8 9 7 5 3 1

FIRST EDITION

Book design by Carole Lowenstein

FRONT ENDPAPER: *President Nixon's letter of resignation, addressed to the
Secretary of State in accordance with the law of presidential succession,
first passed in 1792.*

BACK ENDPAPER: *Richard Nixon's Oval Office in the White House.
He preferred to work in a private hideaway in the
Old Executive Office Building next door.*

PRECEDING PAGES: *Interviewing Richard Nixon for the opening
of his presidential library.*

To Meredith,
always

Who was Richard Nixon?

PREFACE

Just inside the stately columned building that houses the Richard M. Nixon Presidential Library near his boyhood home in Yorba Linda, California, there is a poster-size white-on-black greeting that asks the evocative question: WHO WAS RICHARD NIXON?

From his humble beginnings until his death in 1994 Richard Nixon spent much of his life working and striving, rising and falling and rising again, and always "daring greatly" in whatever arena he entered. The legacy of Richard Nixon's 50 years in the arena—as Theodore Roosevelt called the political world—remains controversial. Was he a peace maker or a warmonger? Did he bring the country together or did he divide it? Did he leave the nation and the world a better place or not?

The answers are far from simple. So as you walk through these galleries, take a moment to step into a President's shoes. Explore Richard Nixon's life and career from the inside and come to your own conclusion. Decide for yourself. Who was Richard Nixon?

That provocative invitation is not far from a stylish gallery recording Nixon's historic visit to China, alongside another that depicts his efforts to ease tensions with the Soviet Union. His bold and very controversial management of the Vietnam war receives dramatic attention.

Then, in a separate corridor, oversize capital letters in bright red: WATERGATE, the scandal that brought him down, presented here in bold candor and unblinking detail. The last year of his presidency, from August 1973 to August 1974, was Richard Nixon's darkest, most indefensible time in the arena.

I was White House correspondent for NBC News during that turbulent time, and recently I've been reflecting on the enduring lessons, high drama, and historic consequences of that fateful year. It is, if you will, a reporter's experience of Watergate, the final act. It is a mix of what I saw, experienced, and concluded as Watergate played out. But it is also a mix of what Bob Woodward and Carl Bernstein learned later in their superb book *The Final Days*. Evan Thomas's post-Watergate reporting for *Being Nixon: A Man Divided* was equally helpful and important. All of this was before electronic social media, before the reporting universe exploded into an expanding mass of fact, speculation, propaganda, and artifice. It is one reporter's personal recollection of a time of great consequence for the nation and for a man who, even in death, provokes the question: Who was Richard Nixon?

THE FALL OF RICHARD NIXON

Police escort demonstrators from the Supreme Court, where
a crowd awaited a ruling on the Watergate tapes.
On the day the Supreme Court ruled,
Nixon appeared to have hit a wall.

INTRODUCTION

This is how the presidential world of Richard Nixon ends.

On July 24, 1974, the president is holed up in San Clemente, California, at La Casa Pacifica, his grand seaside mansion. It is less than an hour south of the president's very modest childhood home in Yorba Linda, the working-class community where he grew up as a bright, awkward, and ambitious child in a Quaker household largely bereft of familial affection.

On this sunny day in late July, the White House press corps is housed in the commodious Surf & Sand, a pricey oceanfront hotel in Laguna Beach. The bucolic setting and sybaritic life in the bar and on the beach make for an unlikely setting in which to deal with the serious issues that brought us here.

As a member of that White House appendage, I am hanging out with my colleagues in a makeshift communications office attached to the hotel. We are awaiting a routine daily briefing from the White House press office on the president's schedule, but our attention is focused on a stately building two miles east of the White House in the nation's capital.

The U.S. Supreme Court.

Eight justices are preparing to announce their decision on one of the most momentous cases in American history. A ninth, Justice William Rehnquist, has recused himself because he was an assistant attorney general during Nixon's first term. The essential question is, Does a president have the right to withhold from Congress tape recordings and other relevant material in a case involving suspected illegal behavior in the Oval Office? It is *the* pivotal issue in the long, complex, and historic case known as Watergate. Simply put, it asks whether the president was an active participant in the cover-up of a burglary that unraveled into a massive conspiracy in which senior White House aides, members of the president's cabinet, higher-ups in the Justice Department, officials of the FBI, and senior members of the president's 1972 campaign for reelection all had a role.

Suddenly the word arrives: eight justices of the high court have voted against the president. He must turn over all relevant material to the special prosecutor investigating Watergate, including tape recordings in which he described what actions he wanted taken. Finally Congress and, just as important, the American people will hear, in his own voice, just what the president wanted. Despite the presidential resistance to the long line of testimony, leaks, and circumstantial evidence leading to this moment, it appears that Mr. Nixon has hit the wall.

Outside the press office I spot James St. Clair, a preeminent Boston lawyer who felt it his civic and legal duty to represent the president in this closing phase. St. Clair is leaning against a rail on a second-story balcony, serenely scanning the fair skies.

"Any comment, Mr. St. Clair?"

"It's a beautiful day, Mr. Brokaw."

Smile.

We are at a signature moment. The judicial branch has just delivered what will amount to a political death sentence to a sitting president. As presidential power has evolved over the course of American history, the presidency has been the most powerful of the three branches of government, with the chief executive exercising wide-ranging authority in domestic and foreign initiatives. That political reality was Richard Nixon's primary defense in the long list of legal challenges to his behavior. The Supreme Court's unanimous decision is now a reminder of the Founding Fathers' wise decision to construct a legal system as a check on political assumption.

In less than two years from his landslide reelection, tough-on-crime Richard Milhous Nixon is on the cusp of being forced from office. He was sworn in for his second term as president of the United States on January 20, 1973, with one of the most overwhelming margins in American electoral history, winning forty-nine of the fifty states, and with an indisputable mandate; now, eighteen months later, he is about to be the first president evicted from office.

It is a surreal setting in which he receives the news.

A glorious sunny day on the California coast, not far from where he began his historic odyssey to the presidency. Now he will receive the fateful news in a seaside villa he purchased during his first term, a conspicuous totem of his journey from the small kit home his father had constructed at the beginning of the century.

His closest political aides from the first term and re-election campaign are elsewhere, awaiting their sentences as convicts in the political scandal. The Nixon men were members of the white-collar Republican establishment, comfortable in country clubs and fraternity houses. They helped lift him to historic highs during his first term and then inexplicably signed on to nefarious, blatantly illegal schemes to fix his reelection against an obviously weak opponent.

By any measurement, it was one of the most bizarre and incomprehensible scandals, political or otherwise. There seemed to be no end to its vaudevillian qualities, which led to this, the U.S. Supreme Court ruling unanimously against the president, leading either to his impeachment or to his resignation.

The irascible gonzo journalist Hunter S. Thompson appeared in San Clemente, demanding that the White House press office arrange for his magazine, *Rolling Stone,* to photograph President Nixon standing on the shoreline of the Pacific Ocean in a blue serge suit and black lace-up shoes—with his back to the sea. The not very subtle message: Richard Nixon has come to the end of his long political life where it started—trapped at the edge of the Pacific on the California coast. The symbolism was not lost on the White House press office, and Hunter was turned down.

I had arrived at this same press office the year before, in the summer of 1973, as the new NBC News White House correspondent, anticipating a challenging turn in my career.

My God, what a year it had been.

We were nearing the end of what was later memorably labeled "our long national nightmare."

FOLLOWING PAGE: *The men around Nixon: Chief of Staff Bob Haldeman, Appointments Secretary Dwight Chapin, Domestic Policy Advisor John Ehrlichman—among the cocksure West Coast tribal team Nixon assembled. Haldeman, Chapin, and Ehrlichman would all go to jail.*

PART I

1973

Former White House counsel John Dean testified before
the Senate Watergate Committee in June 1973. Dean had
already described to Senate investigators what
President Nixon knew about the Watergate burglary.

CHAPTER 1

FOR ALL OF 1973 AND MOST OF 1974, America and the world watched as the fate of the most powerful nation on earth and its familiar president played out on the screen of history and daily journalism. By all expectations, 1973 should have been the beginning of a glorious conclusion to the public life of Richard Milhous Nixon, the poor boy from Southern California who fought his way into the highest offices in America with a brilliant mind, a deep dark streak, and a personality constantly in conflict with the demands of his calling.

He began the year triumphantly, starting to wind down the unpopular Vietnam War as he launched a second term as president with nearly 61 percent of the American electorate having voted for him, a victory for this durable, familiar, and yet enigmatic son of Quaker parents. He had crushed the liberal establishment.

What could go wrong?

It had already gone wrong back in the summer of 1972, when a bumbling gang of burglars working for the Nixon reelection campaign were caught in a clumsy attempt to rifle through files at the Democratic National Committee headquarters in the Watergate Hotel.

Two gifted rookie reporters from *The Washington Post*, Bob Woodward and Carl Bernstein, were assigned to look into the burglary, and as they began to unravel the details, it became clear that this was no ordinary breaking and entering. Piece by piece, they constructed a case that traced the break-in from low-level assistants to the highest tiers of President Nixon's staff. Nixon's closest advisers, cabinet members, and fundraisers were already enmeshed in a spreading scandal that went beyond that botched burglary.

It would forever be known simply as Watergate: the web of lies, payoffs, and toxic tape recordings, followed, finally, by the first resignation of an American president. All of it demanded closer examination.

To this day, the essential question defies a rational answer: Why did the president's men organize a nighttime invasion of the Democratic Party headquarters when they were so far ahead of George McGovern in all the polls?

Later we learned that during his first term, Nixon had made a shady deal with milk producers, supporting higher prices in exchange for campaign contributions. Also, Nixon's fundraisers had blatantly violated new laws designed to provide transparency to campaign contributions. Other Nixon acolytes had written phony letters maligning the character of prominent Democrats.

Nonetheless, Nixon had survived massive demonstrations against his Vietnam policies in his first term, polls showed strong support for the law-and-order tenor of his campaign, his opening to China was widely praised, and the United States and the Soviet Union were negotiating new limits on nuclear weapons.

All the indicators showed Nixon was poised to crush McGovern.

The most tantalizing questions, however, remained: What was President Nixon's role, if any, in the burglary? And were there other dirty tricks yet to be exposed?

The reporting of Woodward and Bernstein continued to raise questions about the involvement of Nixon aides in the nefarious activities, and that went unnoticed by neither the feisty federal judge, John Sirica, who presided over the initial Watergate trials, nor the Democratic majority in the U.S. Senate.

Partly as a result of Sirica's warning that not all the facts had been revealed, the Senate voted unanimously on February 7, 1973, to establish a special committee to investigate Watergate. It was led by Senator Sam Ervin of North Carolina, the very model of a folksy, shrewd, good ol' boy southern lawyer. His Senate Republican counterpart was another southerner, the equally shrewd and likable Howard Baker of Tennessee.

In April 1973, Nixon reluctantly dismissed two of his closest aides, H. R. "Bob" Haldeman and John Ehrlichman; they would soon perjure themselves before the Senate committee by denying their roles in the break-in cover-up. White House counsel John Dean was fired as well, after describing to the Senate investigators what the president knew about the burglary, saying the president was in the room on thirty-five occasions when the Watergate break-in was discussed.

The Senate committee hearings started in May 1973 and quickly became must-see TV for the nation as the cast of once-powerful White House aides struggled to explain how and why the White House, the very symbol of American strength and prestige, could have been involved in such a tawdry enterprise.

Daytime television audiences watching the Senate Watergate Committee during the summer of 1973 were riveted by the country-judge charm of Chairman Sam Ervin and by Howard Baker, who asked, "What did the president know and when did he know it?" While the president was trying to wind down the Vietnam War, strike up a new relationship with the Soviet Union, and capitalize on his historic opening to China, his closest aides were being questioned on Capitol Hill by the Senate committee, igniting time bombs on his future.

One presidential aide, Alexander Butterfield, was called to describe how the White House offices were organized, and he disclosed the unexpected news that an elaborate taping system had been installed to capture historic moments for future archives. It also recorded presidential conversations on subjects Nixon and his advisers presumably didn't expect to become whatever metaphor you like—smoking gun, noose, trapdoor. The recordings quickly became *the* prize in the investigation. Sam Ervin and his fellow senators were determined to get them.

So were Attorney General Elliot Richardson and the special prosecutor Richardson had brought on board,

Archibald Cox, both Harvard men, the kind Nixon privately detested. They had been appointed as the scandal
was heating up.

John Mitchell, Nixon's former law partner and original attorney general, portrayed himself as Mr. Law and
Order, but when he moved over to chair the President's
reelection campaign he became deeply involved in the
Watergate cover-up. He knew about the burglaries and
approved of efforts to get the CIA involved as a cover,
claiming national security. Eventually Mitchell was convicted of perjury, obstruction of justice, and conspiracy.

Richard Kleindienst, Mitchell's successor at Justice,
had failed to tell authorities about President Nixon's
order to ignore an antitrust investigation of the manu-
facturing conglomerate ITT when Kleindienst was an
assistant AG. Later, after Kleindienst had been elevated
to attorney general, he refused a request from G. Gordon Liddy to intervene in the Watergate investigation to
protect CREEP, the President's reelection campaign,
which was deeply involved in the break-in. Kleindienst
resigned as attorney general and returned to his home
state of Arizona to resume his law practice. His replacement was Elliot Richardson, who would come to play a
major role in the President's demise.

By August 1973, several of Nixon's top advisers had lied
their way into certain jail time. The bungled Watergate
break-in was symptomatic of a larger criminal conspiracy run out of the White House, the aim of which was to
crush political enemies.

The fabric of the presidency was unraveling, and constitutional law was under assault. That we've known for some time. What is worth examining again, in light of today's political climate, are the day-to-day developments, decisions, and delusions, as well as the actions of the president, that led to the historic disgrace of the man who came so far and fell so hard.

On August 15, 1973, the president took his case to the American people. He opened his speech with a note of contrition, saying that because the abuses had taken place in his administration he accepted "full responsibility" and the right of the Senate committee to investigate the charges. His most emphatic statement was in his defense:

> I state again to every one of you listening tonight these facts—I had no prior knowledge of the Watergate break-in. I neither took part in nor knew about any of the subsequent cover-up activities. I neither authorized nor encouraged subordinates to engage in illegal or improper campaign tactics.
>
> That was and that is the simple truth.

We now know that if there had been an electronic truth meter in the studio at the time, sirens would have been wailing, horns honking, lights flashing, and an off-screen voice bellowing, "Are you kidding?"

The president went on to describe what he insisted were his many efforts to uncover the facts about the break-in, and then got to the heart of his speech: the right of a president to protect confidential conversations and memoranda.

His speech was designed to advance the case for

presidential authority and to proclaim his innocence, arguments that would be central to his defense for the next year. He argued on national television that the Oval Office tapes were "privileged." In doing so, he invoked, without using the term, the concept of executive privilege, which is reserved for the chief executive of the United States; the concept has evolved with the presidency, and is designed to protect the executive branch from raids, subpoenas, and other interventions by the legislative or judicial branch.

Executive privilege. We would be hearing a lot about that presidential claim in the coming months, even as we do today, as I write this, during the Trump administration. President Nixon argued on that August night that if executive privilege were compromised, "it would cripple future presidents by inhibiting conversations between them and those they look to for advice." The Nixon strategy would undergo many contortions in the coming months, but his fundamental defense was now in place.

*Chief of Staff Bob Haldeman, a master of White House
organization and discipline who was also
a Watergate ringmaster.*

CHAPTER 2

I N AUGUST 1973, ALL OF THIS was playing out against a political reality that on the surface seemed to favor the president. When President Nixon took office for his second term earlier that year, he had an indisputable mandate. Peace talks with the North Vietnamese were making progress. Relations with the Soviet Union had entered a promising new era. China, after Nixon's bold first-term trip, was slowly opening for business.

But by midsummer there were reports of more criminal activities run out of the White House, including a break-in at the office of Daniel Ellsberg's psychiatrist. Ellsberg was the former Marine and Defense Department aide who had famously released to the press a secret and devastating account revealing the greatly flawed government plan for winning in Vietnam dating back to the Johnson administration. The Nixon White House had hoped to find embarrassing information about Ellsberg's mental state in order to discredit him—in a very real sense, abusing its power for the purpose of smearing a private American citizen.

CREEP—to use the popular moniker for the financial wing of President Nixon's Committee for the Re-Election of the President (officially, CRP)—had been run like something out of a John Grisham novel. A heretofore little-known Southern California lawyer, Herb Kalmbach, had set up the fundraising office in Los Angeles and sent out detailed descriptions on how to circumvent campaign finance laws. (One went to my boss at NBC in Los Angeles, and he immediately sent it over to me. Editors at *The Huntley-Brinkley Report* in New York were not interested, so I slipped it to my friend Steve Roberts of *The New York Times* and he had a well-placed exclusive in his paper.)

Before the 1972 election, Kalmbach's luxurious suite of offices had opened in a pricey neighborhood on Wilshire Boulevard. The decor suggested that this was a prestigious firm working on a variety of important legal matters, yet its principal mission was to raise gobs of money for the Nixon campaign. And so it did. The man with his name on the door, Herbert Kalmbach, eventually went to jail for gross violations of campaign finance laws.

By August 1973 these were full-blown scandals, too.

Men who had risen to the top of the White House power grid were suddenly suspects in a chain of events leading to the Watergate break-in. Mistrust now tainted the most powerful figures in the Nixon administration, including chief of staff Bob Haldeman, domestic policy adviser John Ehrlichman, special counsel Charles Colson, and White House counsel John Dean at the top, as well as a string of eager but misguided lieutenants below them: campaign aide Jeb Magruder, appointments secretary Dwight Chapin, Ehrlichman aide Egil Krogh, and political hand Donald Segretti.

Several of the president's closest advisers had not come from the traditional East Coast Republican establishment. They had arrived four years earlier from the West Coast, the political offspring of Californian Richard Nixon. They brought to his first term as president can-do exuberance and little experience in the complex culture of the nation's capital. As they prepared for a second four-year term, they were cocksure and more West Coast tribal than ever.

My friend Zan Thompson, a savvy California Republican political consultant, later captured the attitude of these eager acolytes and the culture they bred in Nixon's White House. In an op-ed in *The New York Times*, she wrote:

When the extent of the dingy little deeds was first becoming known, Herb Klein, who was the White House director of communications, said, "Too much responsibility was given to too many people with no experience."

It was the day of the deadly amateur. The White House was full of people who had "never run for sheriff," who knew nothing of politics, who were "sniffy" little snobs and who had perfectly marvelous teeth. Young men, whose qualifications for White House service were limited almost entirely to blowing up balloons at campaign rallies and seeing that the happy volunteers had buses that ran on time, were suddenly seen striding through the Executive Office Building and the west wing of the White House as though the weight of Government were on their shoulders. Sadly, it was. And what they were all trying to figure out was how to get permission to eat in the White House mess, where the air is rarefied, and they have the Mexican plate on Wednesdays.

Three weeks after I'd started my new job as a White House correspondent for NBC News, a Los Angeles grand jury handed down indictments in the case of the break-in at the office of Daniel Ellsberg's psychiatrist, naming as defendants John Ehrlichman, the president's right-hand man for domestic affairs; Egil Krogh, Ehrlichman's young aide; former CIA operative G. Gordon Liddy; and David Young, an aide to Henry Kissinger. It was the beginning of a series of indictments, confessions, and other accounts of criminal behavior by those closest to President Nixon.

As we experience another chaotic time in the American presidency, it is worth remembering what we went through before.

The role of a White House correspondent during the last year of the Nixon presidency was at once an intense, bewildering, and fascinating professional and personal experience, mixed in, as well, with the Washington journalism culture and a social scene unchanged since the 1950s.

In California, my NBC assignments had been to anchor the 11 P.M. local news and work for the network news on a regular basis. California politics and the cultural upheaval in the state at that time became a personal specialty, and this, in turn, brought visiting reporters to my office.

When David Brinkley arrived to anchor the evening news from California during Ronald Reagan's campaign for governor, I organized a large reel portraying Reagan's evolution as a candidate. It was a daunting assignment for a twenty-six-year-old rookie in the NBC bureau.

David was a demigod, a partner with Chet Huntley in the formation of *The Huntley-Brinkley Report*, the game-changing evening news program that twinned two appealing anchors with a conversational style. They seemed to be inside your living room, delivering the news from a comfortable divan. Watching them during the long night of the 1960 election had settled my career aspirations. "That's what I want to do," I said to myself, and six years later, in a darkened screening room, David was asking me about Ronald Reagan's style. He was always looking for the telling detail.

"How has Reagan changed from movie star to candidate for governor?" he wanted to know.

"Well," I said, "at the beginning of the campaign he appeared in slacks, loafers, and sports jackets, but recently he's been dressed like a CEO, in blue suits."

That night David opened *The Huntley-Brinkley Report* from Los Angeles saying, "Ronald Reagan, who used to be seen around town in slacks and sports jackets, now appears only in suits."

"Good grief," I thought, "what else did I tell him?"

The California political culture was a kind of traveling road show, long on informality, short on rituals and barriers. Which is how I came to know Bob Haldeman before his notoriety as President Nixon's chief of staff.

Before joining the Nixon campaign in 1968, Haldeman had run the Los Angeles office of J. Walter Thompson, the large advertising agency. He was also a regent of the University of California. We met when the new governor, Ronald Reagan, fired Clark Kerr, the university system's president, for being insufficiently tough on widespread student protests.

Haldeman introduced himself and said KNBC, the powerful Los Angeles NBC affiliate, had hired his agency to launch an advertising campaign featuring me as the new face of local television election coverage. He explained that the campaign was in good hands because he had assigned it to one of his young associates at Thompson, Ron Ziegler.

Bob became a reliable source about California Republican party politics. He had been an advance man for Richard Nixon's 1960 presidential bid. When Nixon announced his 1968 campaign, I asked Bob if he was joining up. He quickly responded that he had no plans to go back on the campaign trail. After all, Nixon had not only lost to John F. Kennedy, he had also unwisely run for California governor in 1962 and lost to Edmund G. "Pat" Brown.

Pat Buchanan, Nixon's faithful adviser and speechwriter, remembers with a chuckle, "Then the campaign caught on, and when we got to Oregon, Bob Haldeman showed up with his team and quickly became the manager." Haldeman brought discipline and efficiency as campaign manager, at a critical time; he was rewarded with the powerful position of White House chief of staff when Nixon won the 1968 election. Bob recruited his friend John Ehrlichman to run domestic affairs and his protégé, Ron Ziegler, to be White House press secretary.

In his book *Being Nixon: A Man Divided*, the prize-winning biographer Evan Thomas credits Haldeman with establishing a state-of-the-art White House system that was a model of efficiency for dealing with personnel and political issues. As we learned later, of course, a managerial blueprint is no substitute for sound personal judgment.

Haldeman made his first trip back to California in the spring of 1969. The administration was off to an ambitious start—trying to put more pressure on North Vietnam with massive bombing, which brought on ferocious protests at home, while simultaneously reducing the American troop presence (that fall a lottery system was substituted for the draft) and reaching out to what the Nixon team called "the silent majority," his base of political support.

Haldeman's team called to tell me, "You get an exclusive. You're the only television correspondent on his schedule." Haldeman was accommodating but stern in language and expression. There was no "Hi, how are you?" It was all business.

Before long, it was clear that his brusque demeanor was not personal. He sent an emissary to say that Ron Ziegler was being "promoted" to head the White House communications department. Haldeman wanted me to be the new daily press secretary, and the president had agreed.

Once I recovered, I said, "Tell Bob thank you but sorry," thinking, "No, never, no." I had no interest in leaving journalism for a political job in either party.

Through a third party, Bob kept the offer alive, but finally gave up. My secret held and had a surprise ending.

Henry Kissinger, here addressing assembled journalists in San Clemente, knew how to work the press.

CHAPTER 3

As it turned out, the White House was in my future, only in a different role.

Our family—my wife, Meredith, and our three daughters—had happily settled in as Californians, with weekends at the beach, new friends from the legal, academic, and film communities, affordable housing and entertainment.

Our first home was a prewar custom-built four-bedroom nestled on the rim of a canyon in the San Fernando Valley. We bought it for $42,500. I drove by recently and saw that it had been torn down and replaced by a gated mansion that must be worth three or four million dollars.

John Chancellor, a star reporter headed for the anchor chair at NBC News, would often say, "Come on, Tom, move east and become a grown-up!" It was our private joke, and I'd respond, "John, no thanks. I've gotten used to warm winter days, the beach, and no ties when not on the air."

However, the White House, especially during the growing Watergate scandal, was irresistible. As a family, we gave up the new house on the beach that we had just finished building, the year-round sunshine, the rich mix of friends, the desert, and our weekends in Yosemite and San Francisco, and headed east.

It was a phased-in move, as President Nixon spent the end of August 1973 in San Clemente, and so, when I eased into the White House press pack at the beachfront hotel Surf & Sand in Laguna Beach, I was replacing Richard Valeriani, a longtime friend, who was NBC's new chief diplomatic correspondent, covering National Security Advisor Henry Kissinger. Some of his colleagues in the White House press corps wrote the president of NBC News, arguing that I was not qualified to replace Valeriani at the White House. Dick was unaware of the letter, and in his congenial way he could not have been more gracious in arranging a get-acquainted dinner for me with senior members of the traveling White House press corps.

CBS's Dan Rather returned from a fishing trip to resume his assignment as the best known of that prestigious group of journalists. As he walked in, he was plainly popular with his colleagues, and I felt like the new kid on the first day of school. Dan was immediately cordial with his down-home Texas manners and warm welcome. Over the years, we went head to head on big stories, and later as anchors of our respective flagship broadcasts. We were hotly competitive, but to this day his genial welcome in that first meeting lingers.

In September, President Nixon made a major but not unexpected announcement: Henry Kissinger was named secretary of state. He replaced William Rogers, a long-time Nixon friend, who nonetheless had endured four years of sitting on the sidelines as Kissinger and the president made bold moves on Vietnam, with the Soviet Union, and, especially, with the opening to China.

When Kissinger spoke with the press in his new role, it was striking to see the difference between meeting with him and any encounter the press had with the president. Henry was a master of the reverse compliment. When asked a question about a complicated piece of national security, he'd often say something like "You've framed that very well and opened some options I had not considered." On the plane headed home from an important meeting, Kissinger would organize a small cocktail party for the traveling press and share off-the-record anecdotes or insights. Other members of the Washington press corps referred to the diplomatic correspondents as "the choir boys" for their closeness to Kissinger, a commentary that was part criticism and part jealousy. A few years later, on a flight from Asia, I caught a ride on Kissinger's plane, and when the cocktail hour arrived I didn't claim journalistic sanctity.

*By late 1973, Nixon's White House staff had been
reduced to a handful of loyalists. They included
chief of staff Al Haig, on leave from the Army.
Haig was never far from Nixon's side.*

CHAPTER 4

S TEPPING INTO THE WHITE HOUSE PRESS CORPS as an
outsider meant pedaling hard to establish credibility.
Most days it was a matter of attending the White House
briefing conducted by the amiable Gerald Warren, who
had replaced Ron Ziegler as the daily briefer when
Ziegler was initially dismissive of what he called "a third-
rate burglary." From the beginning, Ziegler had been an
awkward fit as press secretary, an advertising man as the
president's connection to the White House press corps,
mostly veteran newspapermen who had spent a lifetime
in the trenches of hard-core journalism. Ziegler remained at the president's side through resignation and
the retreat to San Clemente, unaware, so far as I know,
that Haldeman originally thought he should be replaced.
By the end he had been press secretary, director of communications, assistant to the president, and presidential
counselor.

As Ziegler's successor for daily contacts with the press, Warren was a pipe-smoking, martini-drinking veteran of *The San Diego Union,* the flagship newspaper of the conservative Copley chain. As press secretary, he reflected the Republican party line in a straightforward manner and had a better feel for the interaction between the press and the White House.

At the time, networks were not allowed to videotape the daily brief except on occasions authorized by the press office. Official Washington was still a newspaper town. (At the Pentagon, the print clique was so strong that television cameras were not even allowed in the press room.) So Dan Rather, Tom Jarriel of ABC, and I would take notes with our print colleagues and transform them into broadcast style, which is more conversational.

We were rarely on the air during the day except for a "stop the presses" kind of story, which meant we had time to work the phones or compare notes with noncompetitive colleagues. When finished with reporting for *NBC Nightly News,* I'd retreat to the NBC booth shared with NBC's peerless radio correspondent Russ Ward and make calls, looking for fresh material for the next morning's *Today* show.

All of that changed when NBC became the first network broadcaster to add a cable outlet, with its voracious appetite for new material twenty-four/seven. Now our White House correspondents are in and out of the briefing room all day and evening, updating the narrative for MSNBC and *NBC Nightly News,* and they can do all of this on the run because of the advent of iPhones and email.

What has not changed is the limited or nonexistent window for lunch, especially for broadcasters. During Watergate, we were as captive to the unexpected as reporters are during the Trump administration. It was not unusual for White House correspondents to develop a kind of buddy system for journalistic and social reasons.

Shortly after arriving in the press room, a fellow midwesterner, Fred Zimmerman of *The Wall Street Journal*, a native of Kansas City, introduced himself. We were unalike in many ways. He was a chess master, a print journalist, droll, a cigarette guy. Chess and tobacco were not on my menu.

He was a print guy. I was a broadcaster, but we generally had the same take on a story line the Nixon team was pushing on any given day, and that led to an informal review of each other's work. *Do you think I have this right? What do you hear from the Hill on this latest move?*

And about once a month we would try for a quick lunch at the Old Ebbitt Grill, a burger joint two blocks from the White House. It was a popular hangout for the young staffers from the nearby Treasury Department.

One day the room went suddenly dead quiet and all eyes turned to the front door. It was John Ehrlichman making an awkward entrance with his son, who appeared to be about ten years old. Here was a man who, a year earlier, had been one of the country's most powerful figures as Nixon's chief of domestic affairs, a White House power player of the first rank. Now he was nervously looking for a table, trying to be a good dad in a room full of people who knew he was going to jail. It was for me an indelible moment, a lesson in the fleeting nature of power abused. It also offered a split image: although Ehrlichman had been instrumental in organizing a raid on the office of Daniel Ellsberg's psychiatrist, at that moment he was just a bewildered father trying to please his son with a hamburger lunch.

Our occasional Fred and Tom lunches would always turn to the question we struggled with daily as the president or his staff tried out a new strategy.

"Fred, this makes no sense," I'd point out.

Fred would cock an eyebrow and say, "Until you remember he's guilty."

Oh, yeah. That.

The John Dean testimony, Haldeman and Ehrlichman's felonious accounts of presidential conversations, and Charles Colson's "take no prisoners" style left little doubt for us that the President was involved.

But that judgment stayed between us. I didn't go on the air at night and deliver the day's White House line, then add, "Remember, he's guilty." Fred didn't insert that opinion into his *Wall Street Journal* dispatches. We did not feel forced, as contemporary Washington journalists may, to react to every "omigod" message from the vast universe of social media—factual, mythical, malicious, or fanciful. In contrast to President Trump, President Nixon was seldom seen and rarely heard.

By late 1973, Nixon's White House staff had been reduced to a handful of loyalists. They included chief of staff Al Haig, on leave from the Army; Ron Ziegler, communications director and, increasingly, a political adviser; Fred Buzhardt, a modest South Carolinian who had the difficult assignment of special White House counsel; Steve Bull, the president's personal aide; Pat Buchanan, a longtime Nixon loyalist and a chief speechwriter; Diane Sawyer, who later became a major star on 60 *Minutes* for CBS and *World News Tonight* for ABC; Frank Gannon, a combination speechwriter and monitor of the popular culture; and Bryce Harlow, who'd worked in the Eisenhower administration and had come out of the private sector to help the president as an adviser and conduit to the press.

For correspondents, the women in the White House press office and the staff of the presidential travel department were the prized ground forces. They were unfailingly cheerful and good-humored as they distributed schedules, typed White House press releases, and set up shop for the press in hotels and on charter planes—often on short notice, as when the president decided to go to, say, Key Biscayne for personal reasons or Paris for the funeral of French president Georges Pompidou.

We were altogether a movable feast, a mix of the president of the United States, his principal advisers, crack security teams, military aides, White House clerical staff, and print and broadcast journalists, along with their photographers and technicians. It sometimes felt like a separate military unit on the move.

*Vice President Spiro Agnew railed against "damned lies"
at a press conference proclaiming his innocence.
Weeks later, he would resign in disgrace.*

CHAPTER 5

I N 1973, THE WHITE HOUSE PRESS CORPS was dominated
by white males from the networks, big newspapers,
and politically oriented magazines, such as *Time, News-
week,* and *The New Republic.* The indomitable Helen
Thomas of UPI, Frances Lewine of the Associated Press,
and Sarah McClendon, a World War II veteran and syn-
dicated journalist, were the only three woman regulars
on the White House beat.

As the scandal widened, President Nixon was unable
to shake the pursuit of investigators, and newspapers
from around the world began shipping their best reporters to Washington. That was how I came to know Simon
Winchester from *The Guardian,* a gifted and prolific
nonfiction author and a cheerful and erudite compan-
ion. The Australians brought their tabloid-journalism
style and new drinking games to the end of a long day,
and pity the American who thought he could stay to the

finish. At closing time they liked to raise a glass and say, "Here's to one for the road," followed by "Here's to one for the ditch across the road," followed by "Here's to the field across the road and the ditch." The BBC's correspondent was a courtly Englishman who, no matter what was going on, left the press room and walked five blocks to a tearoom to have his afternoon cuppa.

Peter Lisagor of the venerable *Chicago Daily News*, probably the best all-around reporter and raconteur and a beloved member of the Washington press corps, was the class favorite. He had a genial manner, a shrewd fix on whatever policy and politics were in play at the time, an endless supply of Washington lore. Lisagor was a man for all seasons as a Washington correspondent. He was a regular guest on public affairs broadcasts, including *Agronsky & Company*, a panel program on PBS featuring newspaper correspondents analyzing the week's news. Peter's commentary was so engaging he was given the Peabody Award, a coveted journalism prize, for his broadcasting work. He liked to tell the story of the best advice he received as a young journalist: a Chicago editor advised him to walk down the middle of the street and shoot out the windows on both sides. He did just that without developing an oracle complex, a know-it-all attitude. And he had an endless store of political anecdotes that drew all of us to his side when he started recalling the early John Kennedy or Nixon years.

Shortly after arriving at the White House assignment, I managed to get some complicated stories on the air in a fashion that attracted Lisagor's attention. He invited me to lunch at his club across Lafayette Square. Turns out, the invitation had not been prompted by journalistic excellence. He laughed and said, "Oh, hell, I brought you here because we need some new members and I figured you had an iron stomach for the food they serve up."

Lisagor's generation of Washington journalists included Hugh Sidey, *Time* magazine's weekly essayist; John Osborne, a veteran magazine editor and writer who wrote a column for *The New Republic* called "The Nixon Watch," a thoughtful series of essays that was admired for its mix of fact and interpretation; and Carroll Kilpatrick, a soft-spoken Alabama native, the *Washington Post* inside man while Woodward and Bernstein were reinventing Washington journalism outside the White House gates.

These veteran journalists were old-school—wise and courteous to a newcomer. They volunteered information on reliable sources and shared stories of other Washington scandals.

Shortly after arriving in Washington, I met Bob Woodward at a cocktail party and wondered whether from time to time he'd be available if I had questions on the White House line of the day against what he was discovering. He agreed and we remain friends.

It was the best of both worlds as Washington journalism was undergoing a generational shift.

(When Lisagor, a World War II veteran, died during the Ford administration, the president arranged for him to be buried at Arlington National Cemetery, and the ceremony included the military tradition of a riderless horse. Peter's wife said if she had known, she would have brought a pair of his Hush Puppies for the stirrups.)

In California, Meredith and I had lived through the rise of Ronald Reagan as governor, Butch and Sundance, the Mamas and the Papas, the Beach Boys, Charles Manson, Mario Savio and Berkeley, O. J. Simpson as football star (not yet as murder suspect), and Bobby Kennedy's assassination. I seldom wore a tie off the air except one night when instructed by a Malibu hostess. Henry Kissinger would be the guest, and our dress was expected to match the occasion. Henry was becoming a Hollywood regular.

With that as a backdrop, the move to Washington in August 1973 was jarring, especially for Meredith, who was giving up a house on the beach for a rental in the August heat of the nation's capital. We quickly understood why, in the 1930s, British diplomats had received a tropical differential for surviving Washington summers, their home offices equating the capital's climate with that of the Amazon.

Fortunately, John Chancellor was moving to New York, and his home on Woodley Road in Northwest Washington was available to rent. It was in a picturesque neighborhood with stately brick homes and towering oak trees. James "Scotty" Reston, the venerated *New York Times* columnist, lived next door; Daniel Schorr of CBS News and Douglas Kiker, my NBC News colleague, were across the street; Elizabeth Drew, then of *The New Yorker*, was around the corner. Senator Walter Mondale of Minnesota lived a block away.

My friend Robert Novak, the conservative columnist, asked where we were living. When I said, "Woodley Road," he scoffed, "You have to pass a saliva test for liberalism to live in that neighborhood!"

Although I'd been coming to Washington for a number of years, I had no full appreciation of the tribalism until we moved in. The social rituals were similar, but the turf was delineated. Georgetown was the home of *Washington Post* publisher Katharine Graham; of Averell Harriman, the wealthy railroad heir, ambassador to the Soviet Union during World Ward II, former Governor of New York, now an elder statesman of the Democratic Party.

Meredith and I were accustomed to California's more casual form of entertaining, but we had an early lesson from our friends George and Liz Stevens, who bridged California and Washington. George had grown up in California as the son of a famous father, George Stevens, Sr., the director of celebrated films such as *Shane* and *Giant*, and come to Washington to run the film division of the United States Information Agency under President Kennedy.

He married Liz, a member of a prominent Virginia family, and together they moved to California, where George started the American Film Institute. They returned to Washington and George established the annual Kennedy Center Honors gala, a celebration of America's legendary artists in film, music, dance, and stage. Liz was an active organizer for the Democratic Party. When we arrived in Washington, they invited us to a welcoming dinner in their Georgetown home.

It was much more of a dress-up affair than we antici-
pated. Alice Roosevelt Longworth, Theodore Roosevelt's
daughter, was a chatty guest in a long dress and repre-
sented how far we'd come from our Southern California
circles. The lively conversation, gossip that transcended
partisan lines, and warm hospitality put us at ease and
formed the foundation of a Stevens-Brokaw family
friendship that continues to this day.

Averell Harriman's wealth, political standing, and
marriage put him atop the liberal Georgetown infra-
structure. He was married to the legendary Pamela, once
Winston Churchill's daughter-in-law and the purported
lover of, among others, William Paley of CBS; Edward R.
Murrow, the immortal CBS News commentator; Gianni
Agnelli, the Italian auto baron; and Baron Elie de Roth-
schild. Pamela had had an earlier affair with Harriman,
and when her marriage to Broadway producer Leland
Hayward ended with his death she reconnected with
Harriman, and together they became a marquee power
couple.

Pamela was born to the roles of courtesan, wife, hostess. Unfailingly charming, she presided over the Harri-
mans' Georgetown home with grace and political savvy.

Somehow we got onto Pamela's radar screen and
were invited to dinner as one of the new young couples
in town.

Two tables of eight with finger bowls, rows of silver,
excellent wines, and entrées served by the graceful house
staff. Guests were usually a mix of Democratic VIPs—
Senators Gaylord Nelson, Hubert Humphrey, Ted Kennedy, or former defense secretary Robert McNamara, or

Bob Strauss, the Texas power lawyer, along with Georgetown pundits like Joe Kraft.

Meredith was impressed by how Pamela smoothly
broke all the new feminist trends by taking the women
upstairs for their own post-dinner tête-à-tête, a much
livelier, richer session than what the men downstairs
were experiencing. Once the men had cigars lit and
brandy glasses filled, Averell would introduce a topic for
discussion, and it was almost always global or economic,
seldom Watergate.

Joe Biden and I have often laughed about the night
when he was the rookie senator and was asked what to
do about the energy crisis brought on by Saudi Arabia.
As he launched into a kind of campaign oration, he
reached for an object in a bowl in front of him and
began nervously tossing it back and forth in his hands as
if it were a baseball. When the session was over, Ted
Kennedy walked over to him and said, "Nice job, Joe,
but next time leave things where they were. That was a
Fabergé egg you were tossing around."

One of our Northwest Washington neighbors invited
us to a "casual" Sunday night supper where the wine was
first-rate, the sterling was heirloom, and the guests were
our age, preppy, and, as I learned, Republicans. When I
made an offhand remark about a White House gaffe, the
host took me aside and, chuckling, said, "We're on the
president's team. I work in the administration."

It was a useful reminder that there was a wide band
of GOP public servants doing their duty without being
worried that the FBI would come calling. The host was
Richard Fairbanks, whose great-grandfather had been

Teddy Roosevelt's vice president. Over the next forty years, Dick served his country in what TR liked to call the arena—as a diplomat, specializing in the Middle East, and as an entrepreneur creating new programs for public service and the environment. He also worked in congressional relations in the Reagan administration. Richard never lost his enthusiasm for new challenges for the public benefit. Sadly, he died of a brain tumor in his early seventies, but I often think of him as someone who worked in the Nixon administration for the public good, not as an obsessed disciple of Richard Nixon.

There are remnants of the Washington dinner-party circuit. The always enterprising Sally Quinn, journalist and widow of hall of fame *Washington Post* editor Ben Bradlee, regularly opens her Georgetown home to authors with new books and for celebrations of birthdays for friends. But the black-tie-and-long-gown evenings of political power brokers have gone the way of four-term senators.

In fact, while Meredith and I enjoyed the occasional glittering social occasion, the seven-day-a-week demands of my job, and for Meredith the twenty-four/seven responsibilities of being mother to three daughters ages four, six, and eight, were daunting. Somehow she managed with grace, good humor, and time to also pursue her role as an instructor in ESL, English as a Second Language. Before long she was admired for her many personal qualities and not as "the wife of. . . ."

Washington has changed in so many ways. Now many members of Congress scoot for their home state when the weekend arrives or use their Capitol Hill office as a bedroom. The vast army of journalists is too busy filing every political utterance, every large or small development, on the endless conveyor belt of digital media.

Arriving in Washington, I was not just stepping off the boat onto a new land, so to speak. While based in California I covered the riotous 1968 Democratic convention in Chicago and the Nixon comeback convention in Miami. Four years later, I was in Miami again for the George McGovern "new" Democratic convention, where the delegates were a much greater mix ethnically, many of them veterans of the unruly antiwar movement. Nixon was renominated as the GOP candidate, also in Miami, in what was essentially a coronation. It was a whiplash experience to go from the counterculture of the Democrats to the country-club GOP. Because of my California experience with Bob Haldeman and my South Dakota connection to Senator McGovern, I had a kind of roaming right in both halls.

As a newcomer to Washington, I wanted to make the rounds and meet not just press secretaries and other staffers but cabinet officers and senior administration officials. NBC colleagues and other friends were gently discouraging. "You really shouldn't bother cabinet officers," they told me. "Just deal with their staff." Nonetheless, my first experience was a memorable moment: a visit with Elliot Richardson, the Boston Brahmin who had replaced Richard Kleindienst as attorney general. Richardson's press secretary was surprised by the request but accommodating. Richardson greeted me cordially while continuing his hobby of drawing or doodling as he talked. I had read about his unusual distraction and asked if he hoped to publish a collection. He offered a small smile and said, "No, I just enjoy this."

After explaining my newcomer status and hopes for staying in touch, I asked a final question: "Anything coming up to be thinking about?" He stopped doodling for just a moment, smiled, knocked on his desk, and said, "No, don't think so."

Two days later, the word began to leak out that Vice President Spiro "Ted" Agnew was under investigation for taking bribes when he was governor of Maryland. Richardson's office was fully involved in the investigation. I'd been a political reporter long enough not to be surprised that Richardson hadn't mentioned anything, but thought my courtesy call still might pay dividends someday.

The Agnew development was completely unexpected. He had not been part of the Watergate tangle, and, of course, if Nixon didn't survive, Agnew would become president.

Agnew decided to fight back against the kickback rumors. He called a news conference at the Old Executive Office Building, commonly known as the EOB. He didn't duck or weave. Regarding the allegations he said, "I'm denying them outright, and I'm labeling them—and I think a person in my position at a time like this might be permitted this departure from normal language—as damned lies."

It turns out his denial was a damned lie, but his performance, especially in the wake of all the ducking, dodging, and weaving of the Watergate principals, received praise from unexpected quarters. *The Boston Globe* called him "a stand-up guy." *The Washington Post* commented on his "skill and some fire . . . frank bluntness." Richard Cohen was a *Washington Post* reporter working on the Agnew investigation, and even he was impressed by the vice president's performance. "I was fully familiar with the charges against him," Cohen wrote, "and believed them to be true. Yet the man was such a stalwart defender of himself that I came to conclude he was a genius at lying. It was quite a performance and it made me, for a second, wonder about his guilt."

Cohen also believes that FBI director J. Edgar Hoover had been aware of Agnew's guilt earlier and, in Hoover-like fashion, thought the vice president would become president because Nixon would be forced to resign. If that were to happen, Hoover would have Agnew in the crosshairs, just as he'd had John F. Kennedy pinned because of his womanizing before becoming president.

Hoover died before the Agnew news became public, but Cohen extended his theory to the number two man at the FBI after Hoover's death, then a little-known FBI lifer named Mark Felt.

Mark Felt, "my friend" in Bob Woodward's early description, is now known as Deep Throat, and as Woodward's important source on Nixon. Felt ultimately went public as Woodward's invaluable informant, but Cohen's personal theory is that Felt had wanted to be made FBI director. Instead, at Hoover's death, Felt was passed over, and he became the shadowy figure familiar from the Robert Redford film on Watergate, meeting Woodward in a D.C. garage and repeatedly saying, "Follow the money," the memorable phrase made up by screenwriter Bill Goldman.

The Agnew TV appearances ended with his indictment. As we have learned so often from Washington scandals, an Oscar-worthy performance proclaiming innocence is no match for the hard evidence of guilt. The federal agents on the Agnew case had an airtight case against "Spiggy," as they referred to him. He had been taking payoffs through his tenure as county executive, governor, and even as vice president. The "damned lies," as he'd called the original reports, turned out to be damning but not lies.

In late September, he told a Los Angeles audience, "I will not resign if indicted." Eleven days later, he stood before a federal judge in a Baltimore courtroom and admitted that he had evaded federal income tax on a payment of $29,500 he'd received as governor of Maryland in 1967. Simultaneously, he sent Secretary of State Henry Kissinger a brief statement under the provisions of the Succession Act: "I hereby resign the office of Vice President of the United States effective immediately."

Federal Judge Walter Hoffman sentenced Agnew to three years' probation and a fine of $10,000 in an arrangement worked out with the Justice Department. Judge Hoffman wanted to send Agnew to prison, but Attorney General Richardson intervened, saying, "Leniency is justified." Agnew and President Nixon had an awkward exchange of letters, with the president—who addressed his VP as "Dear Ted"—praising his patriotism and dedication but concluding that Agnew's decision to resign was advisable.

For the first time, the Twenty-fifth Amendment to the Constitution kicked in, requiring the president to find a successor as vice president who would be acceptable to the Senate and the House of Representatives. Both chambers were controlled by Democrats, so the choice could not be overtly ideological. Ten months into Richard Nixon's second term, less than a year after his landslide victory, his closest aides were either standing by for their sentencing or about to be found guilty. Now that his vice president was leaving in disgrace, it was important for the president to make a safe, solid, and squeaky-clean choice for a replacement. His criteria were that it had to be a Republican, share his views on foreign policy, and be able to work with both parties in Congress.

The guessing game began immediately. Likely candidates seemed to be Governor Nelson Rockefeller of New York (who would get his turn as vice president with Gerald Ford); John Connally, a former Democrat and governor of Texas, said to be a Nixon favorite; George H. W. Bush, chair of the Republican National Committee; and Congresswoman Margaret Heckler of Massachusetts. John Wayne wrote the president recommending California governor Ronald Reagan, arguing that he was "the most untarnished and honorable American leader in politics."

The president asked House minority leader Gerald Ford of Michigan to canvass his Republican colleagues for recommendations. By October 11, the president had an enormous stack of suggestions. He retreated to Camp David to make his choice. Gerald Ford, the party stalwart, was one of the top three choices of more than a hundred Republicans in the House and Senate—a safe, reliable, and scandal-free candidate.

The president returned to the White House the next morning, and shortly thereafter David Broder, the political reporter for *The Washington Post*, learned that Jerry Ford, as he was widely known, was the president's choice. (Broder's reputation was so impeccable that other reporters knew they could safely say, "I've been able to independently confirm Congressman Ford will be nominated for vice president.")

Nixon and Israel's prime minister, Golda Meir, met in the Oval Office following the Yom Kippur War, which might have been fatal to Israel's survival had President Nixon not stepped in with Operation Nickel Grass. Meir called Nixon "my president."

CHAPTER 6

WATERGATE AND SPECULATION about the president's future continued to permeate Washington. The 1973 summer hearings and Woodward and Bernstein's almost daily chronicle of new developments, the Agnew resignation, and the president's defensive crouch gave an otherwise beautiful autumn an air of uncertainty and foreboding.

The president, his family, and his aides were constantly engaged in efforts to demonstrate that Watergate was an obsession of the Washington press and Nixon's enemies. In early October, the NBC news office called to say that the president and Mrs. Nixon were dining at Trader Vic's, the faux-Polynesian restaurant just across Lafayette Square from the White House. They were joined by daughter Julie, son-in-law David Eisenhower, and friends Cynthia and Robert Milligan.

The president was in a jolly temperament as he exited. It was an open secret in political circles that Nixon didn't handle alcohol well. It seemed he may have had too many of Trader Vic's signature rum drinks with the tiny umbrellas as decoration. He looked as gregarious as I had ever seen him as he chatted with the Saudi ambassador to the United States and a party of Italian tourists, confiding to them that he planned a trip to Europe in the spring. Plainly he was trying to convey a "What, me worry?" persona to anyone watching.

October, the month of Halloween, was day after day, week after week, thirty-one days of triumph and trial for the president, an unrelenting challenge to his reputation as a global statesman, as well as his determination to hold off impeachment and keep his chair in the Oval Office. Of all the months of his presidency, October 1973 was his greatest test on so many levels.

It began with the Russian-backed surprise attack on Israel by Syrian and Egyptian forces on Yom Kippur, the holiest day on the Jewish calendar. The news was particularly startling because Israel had uncharacteristically been caught completely off guard. The coordinated pincer attack by Syria and Egypt was so effective in its early stages that the unthinkable was now possible: Israel could be seriously, maybe fatally damaged. What is now largely overlooked in any recounting of that time is that Nixon was operating in the arena he loved most: the great game of international power moves.

The Soviets obviously thought this was a time to exploit America's preoccupation with Watergate by backing the war on Israel. The Israelis needed help, fast. Nixon and Secretary of State Henry Kissinger were now in their element. This was not about burglaries and bribes. This was a showdown with Moscow over the survival of America's most important friend in the always volatile Middle East.

Golda Meir, Israel's prime minister, sent an SOS to the White House for immediate military and diplomatic help. Nixon and Kissinger recognized an opportunity to shut the Soviets out of the Middle East if Israel, with American help, could prevail. They organized a massive airlift of a wide range of military supplies to Israel, intending to start with commercial air carriers, followed by military aircraft. When, initially, there was some confusion in the U.S. Defense Department about how to organize the airlift Nixon had ordered, he cut to the chase, barking, "Goddam it, use every [plane] we have. Tell them to send everything that can fly."

The rearmament effort was called Operation Nickel Grass, and it quickly evolved into a massive American military operation, because U.S. commercial carriers didn't want to become part of a war. Most European nations wanted no part of the hastily arranged mission either, so the administration made a deal with Portugal to use one of its bases on the Azores Islands. Almost overnight, more than thirty American military flights a day began landing there and refueling for the next hop into Israel, carrying tanks, artillery, ammunition, and other supplies. For the last leg, the dangerous flights into Israel, U.S. and Israeli fighter escorts flew precise patterns so that other nations would not become aroused. In all, the United States launched 567 air-supply missions to Israel.

And it worked.

Israel went on the offensive, and when the Israeli

forces counterattacked Egyptian troops in the Sinai Desert, the gateway to greater Egypt, and successfully held off Syrian gains in the Golan Heights, the tide turned.

The war was not a minor skirmish. It went on for nearly three weeks. More than two thousand Israeli soldiers were killed and more than seven thousand Egyptians and three thousand Syrians. Without the massive and timely aid from America, Israel would have suffered much larger losses in lives and standing. Golda Meir later called Nixon "my president."

The Soviets effectively abandoned that part of the Middle East, and the Egyptians turned to the United States, eventually making a deal with Israel during the Jimmy Carter administration.

By then Nixon was gone.

While the bold and imaginative rescue was underway, it was not adequately appreciated by America's political and press culture, consumed as we were by Watergate.

Nixon was subjected to an even greater slight when Kissinger and Le Duc Tho, the North Vietnam emissary to the Vietnam War peace talks, were awarded the Nobel Peace Prize for initiating the agreement, eventually leading to the end of that heinous war. The president issued a gracious statement of congratulations, but it is not idle conjecture to imagine that he was wounded, and not hard to imagine him thinking that this was just one more in a lifetime of perceived slights. He comes to the aid of Israel, he is shut out of the Nobel Peace Prize, and all he has left at the end of the day are more demands from special prosecutor Archibald Cox for the June 1972 Watergate tapes, tapes that he knows are toxic for his future.

During October 1973, *The New York Times* was publishing big banner headlines almost daily: ARABS AND IS-RAELIS BATTLE ON TWO FRONTS; ISRAEL REPORTS SUEZ SETBACK, GOLAN GAIN; AGNEW QUITS VICE PRESIDENCY; GERALD FORD NAMED BY NIXON; NIXON TO KEEP TAPES DE-SPITE RULING; NIXON AGREES TO GIVE TAPES TO SIRICA; NIXON DISCHARGES COX FOR DEFIANCE, ABOLISHES WATER-GATE TASK FORCE; U.S. FORCES PUT ON WORLDWIDE ALERT LEST SOVIET SEND TROOPS TO MIDEAST.

As I was reviewing these front pages of *The New York Times,* an item below the fold on Tuesday, October 16, 1973, caught my eye.

MAJOR LANDLORD ACCUSED OF ANTIBLACK BIAS IN CITY

The Department of Justice, charging discrimination against blacks in apartment rentals, brought suit in Federal Court . . . yesterday against the Trump Management Corporation, a major owner and manager of real estate here.

The corporation, which owns and rents more than 14,000 apartments, . . . was accused of violating the Fair Housing Act of 1968. . . .

Donald Trump [yes, that Donald Trump], president [of the family real estate business], denied the charges. . . .

"We have never discriminated," he said, "and we never would. . . . We proved in court that we did not discriminate."

The article noted that Donald Trump's father, Fred Trump, was the principal stockholder and chairman of the Trump Management Corporation. The son was just beginning to make his reputation as a flamboyant playboy with outsize ambitions; he was moving from the outer boroughs into Manhattan. His future as a president of the United States was as unlikely as his claim that his father's company didn't discriminate against black tenants.

Stanley Pottinger, the assistant attorney general of the Civil Rights Division of the Justice Department, recalled that Trump had turned to his friend Roy Cohn for help. Cohn had been the notorious counsel for Joe McCarthy, the Wisconsin senator who insisted the federal government was in the grips of a Communist takeover. McCarthy was eventually disgraced, but Roy Cohn moved to New York and set up shop as a full-service hatchet man. He met Trump on the social circuit and agreed to handle the housing discrimination charges. Pottinger remembers that Cohn was a blowhard but not much of a lawyer, and the Trump organization eventually signed the consent decree, which promised an end to discriminatory practices without admitting guilt.

Forty-five years later, Trump had other lawyers and a different set of problems. In 1973, however, the Trump company was small change in the news of the day.

The war in the Middle East was an Israeli victory, but it had immediate consequences for the United States. Saudi Arabia was threatening an oil boycott as punishment for America's support of Israel, a threat that became a reality and a major disruption for the American economy and day-to-day way of life.

Meanwhile, Watergate was *the* preoccupation of the political, judicial, and press communities in Washington. Archibald Cox, the Watergate special prosecutor, continued to demand tape recordings of Oval Office conversations. So did federal judge John Sirica, the diminutive jurist with a big reputation for legal combat, who was presiding over Watergate issues on the federal bench in the D.C. courthouse.

In the White House, the president was spending more time alone in the living quarters. Later we learned that he would sit alone in an easy chair well past midnight, contemplating how he could manage this crisis, this turn from a landslide electoral victory to a web of staff criminal activity, plus the legal and political pursuit of his role in all of it.

Through friends I met an administration arms analyst on the national security team who unexpectedly provided some insight into the president's state of mind. He shared an experience with a recent memo from the Oval Office.

He said the president's signature was so cramped it was almost illegible, and he'd wondered if it was authentic. He had taken it to secure files that contained other presidential signatures and compared them. He had finally decided that the latest one was real but the work of someone under a lot of stress.

During that fall the White House press rarely saw the president in public appearances, and when we did he often seemed distracted, and with good reason. The attacks and fresh questions about his Watergate role were unrelenting.

George Meany, the powerful head of the AFL-CIO

when organized labor was still a muscular force in American politics, went after Nixon with blunt verbal force. He accused the president of creating a "dark shadow of shame over the spirit of America," adding, "Never in history has a great nation been governed so corruptly." The AFL-CIO convention called for Nixon to resign or the members would demand his impeachment.

Nixon's deputy director of communications was a burly former *Washington Post* reporter who liked to convey a tough-guy posture. Ken Clawson made it clear that he thought that as the new guy I was easy pickings, "just another pretty-face TV reporter from California." But when he asked if I wanted to interview Pat Buchanan as a White House responder to George Meany, I thought, "Why not?"

The president had a speech scheduled to explain his position on Judge Sirica's demands for the Watergate recordings, so a response to Meany was relevant. It was to be the first Nixon speech since the White House had promised that it would no longer recruit in advance friendly voices to call the White House switchboard at a speech's conclusion to rave about its effectiveness.

I had a good relationship with Buchanan. He was an ideological warrior but with an Irish sense of humor and a built-in encyclopedia of American political lore. As head of the White House speechwriting team and a longtime Nixon aide, he was often called on as responder to criticism of the president.

When the Buchanan interview was over, Clawson sent me to a spare office with a phone and a desk bare except for a staff memo face up. It outlined in detail how organizations supportive of the president would call in right after the speech to rave about it. The fix was in, despite the earlier promises not to stuff the ballot box, so to speak.

I immediately thought, "Clawson is trying to set me up. He wants me to take the bait so he can claim it's not true." After memorizing the memo and returning to the NBC cubbyhole in the White House press room, I telephoned one of the organizations on the list.

"Hey, it's the White House. You guys all set with the call-in after the president's speech tonight?"

"Yessir, we have the phone bank all set up."

"Good deal." *Click.*

My next call was to the *Nightly News* producer in New York. I said, "I think I have something more newsworthy than Buchanan's response to Meany." When the story hit the air that night, Clawson was livid.

Turns out the memo had not been a baited trap. It had just been carelessly discarded in an empty office.

My relationship with Buchanan remained intact, however, and a few months later he was my guest at what then was a big deal in Washington, the annual Radio and Television Correspondents' Association Dinner. The broadcast industry staged a black-tie affair that was entertaining but appropriate compared to the now well-known and overbaked White House Correspondents' Dinner, which is carried live on cable television and features celebrity guests, including one year Kim Kardashian, a choice that mystifies me still.

During the week of the Radio and TV dinner, Pat

chose to level another of his flamethrower assaults on the networks for their news coverage of Watergate. As we approached the NBC cocktail party hosted by Julian Goodman, the president of NBC, I suggested to Pat that he wait outside while I cleared the way. Julian, an affable Kentuckian wise in the ways of Washington as a former NBC News bureau chief in the capital, greeted me warmly until I mentioned that Pat was my guest

"I heard you brought that SOB," he said, his face reddening.

Retreating, I told Pat, "We'd better find another place to have a drink."

He laughed and agreed.

The night was a success, if for no other reason than the table at which I was seated. It included the elegant and widely respected Senator Phil Hart of Michigan, a Democrat who had admirers and friends in both parties. From across the table he was smiling at me.

"Mr. Brokaw," he said, "how old are you?"

"I'm thirty-four, Senator," I replied.

He smiled again and shook his head slightly, saying, "That's just great."

Senator Hart died of cancer less than three years later, the day after Christmas, at the age of sixty-four. Hart was known in both parties as the conscience of the Senate for his unassailable integrity and deep commitment to the great social issue of the day, civil rights. He was accorded the singular honor of having a new Senate office building named for him in his dying days.

That night when we had a brief exchange across a banquet table, I did not know he had been a lieutenant colonel in World War II who'd earned a Purple Heart for wounds received while leading troops ashore in Normandy on D-Day. Shipped home to recover from his injuries, he was placed in a hospital ward with two strangers, Army infantrymen who had been grievously wounded in the hard-fought Italian campaign: Bob Dole of Kansas and Danny Inouye of Hawaii. Dole remembers that they spent a lot of nights during their convalescence talking about their futures. They decided public service would be a definitive calling in their civilian lives. Hart, Dole, and Inouye later had a reunion when all three were elected to the U.S. Senate from their respective states, Hart and Inouye as Democrats and Dole as a Republican.

War and the lessons learned brought together Hart, this man of privilege from Michigan; Dole, a small-town kid from Kansas; and Inouye, a Japanese American from Hawaii. As Inouye left for the war, he heard his father say, "This has been a good country for our family. Never dishonor your country. Never dishonor your family. And if you must die in battle, die in honor."

That night in Washington was twenty-five years away from their recounting of their stories in *The Greatest Generation*, but to this day I treasure the memory of Senator Hart.

Whenever I go to the Hart Senate Office Building, I hear him saying, "That's just great."

*Months before Special Prosecutor Archibald Cox (center) was
fired in the Saturday Night Massacre, he had been chosen
by Attorney General Elliot Richardson (right)
to lead the investigation.*

CHAPTER 7

POLITICAL AND LEGAL PRESSURE on the White House
continued to escalate. Judge Sirica and the Democrats in Congress pressed the president for the Watergate tapes. He continued to resist, claiming executive
privilege.

As the feud between the president and special prosecutor Archibald Cox was heating up, Rod and Carla
Hills, friends from California, called. They would be in
Washington and wanted to have dinner. The Hills were
partners in a prestigious Los Angeles law firm headed by
Charlie Munger, Warren Buffett's alter ego. At a time
when women were mostly second-class citizens in blue-
ribbon law partnerships, Carla, a Stanford and Yale Law
honors graduate, was widely regarded as a star in the
high-profile and ultracompetitive California legal culture. Her husband, Rod, another Stanford grad, had
clerked at the U.S. Supreme Court and was equally admired for his legal and political skills.

We met for dinner in Georgetown and Carla confided that Attorney General Richardson had offered her a prestigious post as head of the Justice Department's Civil Division. But would it make sense to give up their golden life and prosperous practice in Southern California to join the Nixon administration? They were well aware of the growing tensions between the Justice Department and the White House, although Richardson had assured them that Carla would be walled off from that political dispute.

What did I think? I encouraged her to accept, saying that now more than ever the country needed qualified people in the important roles, offering to call senior Washington hands to get their reactions. The survey was unanimous: we needed the likes of Carla for the good of the country. So Rod and Carla found a home in the District, put down a deposit, and returned to California to wrap up their professional and personal business before making their big move to Washington and an exciting new job for Carla.

Meanwhile, the tensions between the Oval Office and special prosecutor Cox grew greater every day. Pat Buchanan made no secret of his thoughts: Cox should be fired.

As Pat later wrote in *Nixon's White House Wars,* "I sent Nixon a 1,500-word 'Administratively Confidential' memo . . . urging him to destroy the tapes, fire Cox, and launch a counteroffensive to save his now-imperiled presidency." Buchanan said that "the bonfire of the tapes 'should be announced, not in advance, but as a fait accompli.'" He saw Cox and his "Army . . . like a loose cannon lurching around the deck of a wooden ship." Mixing his metaphors, Buchanan urged the president "to kill the viper in its crib."

Nixon called in his chief of staff, Al Haig, and chief legal counsel, Fred Buzhardt, who disagreed with Pat. They saw his recommendation as the destruction of evidence. The Buchanan memo was written in July 1973. Three months later, the tapes had become so toxic and the president so resistant to demands for them that the stage was set for a monumental showdown with Attorney General Richardson and special counsel Archibald Cox.

Elliot Richardson, with his elite Boston background, was never a natural in the Nixon circle, wanting to be loyal but increasingly concerned about the president's intentions. Richardson had brought to Washington his fellow Harvard alum Archibald Cox, who, with his tweed suits, bow tie, and crew cut, was the epitome of a New England establishment lawyer-professor.

In mid-October, Richardson made a clandestine trip to the White House, where Al Haig, by now the president's chief strategist, proposed a compromise: Nixon would listen to the tapes and arrange for transcripts for Judge Sirica, cutting out Cox. That was a nonstarter for Richardson. He reminded Haig and White House counsel Fred Buzhardt that, during his confirmation hearings, he had promised the Senate Judiciary Committee that he would remove a special prosecutor only for "extraordinary improprieties." Richardson left the White House angry.

A short while later, Haig called with a new proposal:

the president had agreed to a plan to have Mississippi senator John C. Stennis listen to the tapes and sign off on their transcripts. Stennis was hard of hearing and a staunch conservative, but for some reason Richardson didn't immediately object. However, his staff back at Justice convinced him that he was being set up.

Richardson took the plan to Cox, who had reservations but agreed to the plan if the tapes involved were the ones that had been subpoenaed by a grand jury, as requested by the special prosecutor. Cox also wanted Richardson and the White House to understand that he reserved the right to ask for other evidence. When Richardson took that proposal back to the White House, he was blocked in no uncertain terms by Haig and the legal team. If it came to firing Cox, they argued, the public would understand that the president had a right to defend the presidency against inappropriate demands. As we now know from retrospectives on that critical time, Richardson went home and began to outline why he felt obliged to resign.

None of this was known to the White House press at the time, but the next morning I called a source in the White House congressional relations office. He had been briefed on the machinations of the day before and cheerily told me that Richardson had been at the White House and a compromise had been worked out.

Really?

When was this?

Last night or this morning. He wasn't sure.

Good God, this was a major development.

It was early, so I was one of the few reporters already at work. I strolled up to Ziegler's office, where he was drinking coffee out of the White House china cup he always insisted on. I said, "So Richardson was here yesterday and not happy but turned around? How did that happen, Ron?"

The china cup rattled as he hurried it back onto the saucer and said, "Come on. We're going to see Haig."

In Haig's office Ziegler said simply, "Brokaw knows about Richardson's visit and that he was unhappy."

It was my first one-on-one with Haig. He came around the desk and said, "Oh, it's all been worked out. We talked this morning. Elliot likes a drink, you know"—Haig mimicked someone hoisting a glass—"and he told me this morning he's feeling better. We can work something out. Not to worry."

When I pressed for the new arrangement, he said something to the effect of "Not yet. We'll let you know."

Since it was our first personal meeting, he asked how I was getting along in my new assignment.

"Well, General, it's like learning to ski in an avalanche."

That drew a chuckle from Haig, who, after all, was skiing in an avalanche all day, every day.

Haig was confident Richardson was now open to the Stennis option.

Wrong.

As we know now, Cox would not accept the constraints on his mandate and made that clear to Richardson, who understood. It was a Friday night, the eve of one of the most dramatic Saturdays in White House history. The tempo leading to a historic showdown was speeding up.

Saturday morning I was leaving Washington for my weekly commute to New York and the weekend *NBC Nightly News* as Archibald Cox was preparing to give his side of the story in an appearance at the National Press Club. Weekends were often thin on important news, but this weekend promised to be different. Cox, with his salt-and-pepper crew cut, still the special prosecutor, was all charm and tweedy manners.

"I'm certainly not out to get the president of the United States," he said in an Ivy League classroom tone at the Press Club. "I am even worried . . . that I'm getting too big for my britches," he added—a touch of self-deprecation from this New England model of establishment pedigree.

But he made clear that he knew that his brief compelled him "to stick by what I thought was right."

The president was not amused. He wanted Cox fired. When Elliot Richardson had gone to the White House late Saturday afternoon, we later learned, Nixon had told Haig, "If Elliot feels he has to go with his Harvard boy, then that's it."

Richardson informed the president that he was resigning because he would not fire Cox.

Nixon responded, "Let it be on your head," pointing out that this decision came as the Soviets were looking for division in America while the Middle East war was still under way.

Pat Buchanan said, "Nixon didn't want Brezhnev, the Soviet leader at the time, to think Cox could push him around, so he decided to fire Cox."

Richardson, who had been a decorated combat medic during the Normandy invasion in World War II, was not intimidated. He told the president, "I can only say that I believe my resignation is in the public interest."

As we know, Nixon reached the number two man at Justice, William Ruckelshaus, and gave the same order—fire Cox—and got the same response. Ruckelshaus refused and resigned.

Next up was Robert Bork, a conservative former Yale Law professor who was solicitor general. Bork said later that he disagreed with the president's decision but concluded that Nixon did have the authority, so he wrote Cox a letter, dismissing him.

I'm not sure who first used the phrase "Saturday Night Massacre," but it stuck.

In New York Dan Rather, who anchored the Saturday *CBS Evening News,* and I led our broadcasts with the news of the president's actions, then raced to LaGuardia to get the last shuttle to Washington. As we boarded we saw the sage of CBS News, Eric Sevareid, sitting in an aisle seat with other passengers crowding around, asking what was going on. Eric said he really couldn't talk about it and then came back to Dan and me and asked, "What the hell happened?" He was returning from a speaking engagement in New England and didn't have a clue. But by suggesting to other passengers that the story was too big to share, he preserved his reputation as an oracle.

In Washington the scene at the Justice Department

was cinematic. Stanley Pottinger, the assistant attorney general for Civil Rights, told me recently that no one knew quite what to expect. He said two FBI agents appeared to secure the offices. They surveyed the scene of white-collar workers looking on and decided on a low-key approach. They kept their weapons visible but holstered as they went to Richardson's office. The now ex–attorney general greeted them cordially and invited them in.

Arriving in Washington, I went directly to the White House lawn for an 11:30 P.M. special report anchored by John Chancellor, who opened by saying, "The country tonight is in the midst of what may be the most serious constitutional crisis in its history."

Later Pat Buchanan, history buff and press monitor, wrote that in fact the Confederacy breaking away from the Union was much more consequential.

Fred Emery, a British journalist with an English ear for the tabloid punch, went further, saying, "The whiff of the Gestapo was in the clear October air." In Washington a birthday-party tennis tournament for humor columnist Art Buchwald ended in a clatter of abandoned rackets as journalists raced to reporting assignments.

Press Secretary Ron Ziegler was cool and confident, saying the president had made a defensible decision in firing special prosecutor Cox, who had ignored direct orders from the commander in chief. That was not what we were hearing from Republicans as well as Democrats on Capitol Hill and across the country. It was a firestorm of condemnation of Nixon's action.

At midnight, when we wrapped up, Ziegler stood at the diplomatic entrance, waiting for a White House car to take him home. He was smoking a pipe and waved good night convivially before being driven off. I distinctly remember thinking, "Does he really believe this firing of Cox is a victory for the president?" That thought would keep coming back to me in the coming months.

The next morning, Sunday, as luck would have it, I was making my inaugural appearance on *Meet the Press.*

For years it had been the premier Sunday morning public affairs broadcast, direct from the nation's capital. Lawrence Spivak was the stern but fair choirmaster directing a panel of correspondents. I had met him only briefly when first arriving in Washington. That Sunday morning he got right to the point: "Mr. Brokaw, you'll ask the first question. It is very important we get off to a fast start. Do you want to share your opening question with me?"

I said, "I'd rather not, Mr. Spivak. I think it is a good one, and I don't want viewers to think I shared my question with you in advance."

Looking back, that made no sense; nevertheless, Spivak, startled, said, "Okay, but remember, off to a fast start."

Mel Laird, the former secretary of defense and a canny GOP warrior, had been booked in advance, and he could not have been happy about unexpectedly dealing with a political massacre. Larry, as I came to call Mr. Spivak, introduced the program by summarizing Laird's political VIP status and then leaned forward, looked at me sternly, and said, "We will have the first question from Tom Brokaw of NBC News."

I was ready. "Mr. Laird, let me briefly summarize all

that has happened this weekend. The president has ignored an order from the federal appeals court [to turn over tapes]; he has fired the special prosecutor, Archibald Cox; he has accepted the resignation of Attorney General Elliot Richardson; and he has forced the resignation of Deputy Attorney General William Ruckelshaus. In view of all that, don't you expect now that impeachment proceedings against the president will begin in the House of Representatives?"

Spivak leaned back in his chair and smiled. It was the beginning of a wonderful friendship, equaled only when my friend the late Tim Russert took over *Meet* and expanded on the Spivak legacy.

For his part, Laird, always a nimble pol, gave a long-winded answer concluding with the assertion that Congress would find that the president had complied with everything the courts had asked.

Immediately following *Meet the Press*, I went to the headquarters of the special prosecutor, where a posse of reporters had gathered to see what would happen next. James Doyle, a Pulitzer Prize–winning reporter who was Cox's public affairs officer, was in a feisty mood as reporters quizzed him about the White House justification for firing Cox. He said, "If they announce the sky is green and you look up and see the sky is blue . . ." He didn't have to finish the sentence to get his point across.

Federal agents were guarding the entrance to the Justice Department, but Doyle was determined to keep the offices open. So he showed his Justice Department pass and ushered his fellow employees in to demonstrate that the office was still in business.

When the Saturday Night Massacre blew up in the president's face, Buchanan understood that the move to fire Cox had been a disaster. Pat told me, "I called a friend in St. Louis and told him, 'There will be a petition for impeachment on the House floor by Monday.'"

In the chaos of the weekend, I had forgotten Rod and Carla Hills, whom I had encouraged to make the move to Washington. On Monday morning they sent a brief message:

"Thanks a lot, Tom!"

Later Carla explained that they had sold their Los Angeles home, left their prosperous firm, and arrived in Washington the Thursday before the Saturday Night Massacre. When the news broke, they headed back to Los Angeles. Robert Bork, now the acting attorney general, urged Carla to return and take charge of the Justice Department's Civil Division.

President Nixon went on to name Senator William Saxbe, an unimaginative son of Ohio, as the new attorney general. When Carla met with him and asked about her hiring authority, Saxbe startled her by saying, "Mrs. Hills, is it your intention to hire only women?" Carla says she was stunned but found solace from Larry Silberman, Saxbe's deputy, who protected her right to hire whomever she needed.

Rod and Carla soon became pillars of the Washington Republican establishment. She would be elevated to secretary of the Department of Housing and Urban Development when Gerald Ford was president and would later co-chair the prestigious Council on Foreign Relations. Rod would become chair of the Securities and Exchange Commission during the Ford administration.

Carla and I still laugh about her "Thanks a lot, Tom!" message.

"Don't get the impression that you arouse my anger. . . .
You see, one can only be angry with those he respects,"
Nixon told the gathered reporters
at his press conference.

CHAPTER 8

I N THE WHITE HOUSE, the president was surrounded by his tape recordings of Oval Office conversations, but what did they contain? What next for the embattled president?

Nixon decided to take his case to the public with a televised news conference on October 26. He was on the offensive from the beginning as reporters asked him questions. He was asked about an earlier comment he'd made, back in 1968; he had written that he believed that too many shocks to a country can drain it of its energy and stunt its progress.

The president said, "This is a very strong country, and the American people . . . can ride through the shocks."

Then this: "I have never heard or seen such outrageous, vicious, distorted reporting in twenty-seven years of public life." (Sound familiar?)

And: "When people are pounded night after night

with that kind of frantic, hysterical reporting, it natu-rally shakes their confidence."

Then, in typical Nixon style, he assured everyone that "these shocks will not affect me and my doing my job."

This was my first time at a televised news conference as NBC's White House correspondent, and I was quickly flipping through a mental notebook, looking for a fol-low-up question for Nixon, but Robert Pierpoint, the CBS correspondent, came up with just the right one: "You say after you have put on a lot of heat, that you don't blame anyone. I find that a little puzzling. What is it about the television coverage . . . that has so aroused your anger?"

The president responded, "Don't get the impression that you arouse my anger."

Then he added the latest in the long-running Nixon knife fight with the American press: "You see, one can only be angry with those he respects."

Later Ron Ziegler told me that the president had been instructed to call on me because I was a newbie. It's just as well he was otherwise preoccupied. I would have other opportunities, including the last question asked of him at a formal news conference.

*Iranian ambassador Ardeshir Zahedi
with Elizabeth Taylor.*

CHAPTER 9

DESPITE THE SATURDAY NIGHT MASSACRE, the war in the Middle East, the resignation of Vice President Agnew, the special prosecutor's demands for the tapes, and jockeying among the White House, the House, and the Senate, the Washington social merry-go-round did not stop.

One of the fixtures on the Washington social scene was Ardeshir Zahedi, the Iranian ambassador to the United States, a debonair bachelor closely connected to the shah of Iran. Zahedi had an unusual background: he was an Iranian aristocrat with down-home American experience. A graduate of Utah State University's College of Agriculture, he had a degree in animal science.

But as the Iranian ambassador, he was all silk and black tie, a genial if flamboyant host of parties where he connected glittering Hollywood stars with titans of Capitol Hill. At one reception, he introduced Liza Minnelli to Elliot Richardson, and the actress Julie Newmar took turns dancing with Deputy Secretary of State Ken Rush and New York senator Jacob Javits.

Somehow Meredith and I wound up on his invitation list, and the evening was memorable for the elegance of the table settings, the bipartisan mix of guests, and the large crystal bowls of prime Iranian caviar. The caviar factor was not incidental, especially for the guests who were favored the next day with a limousine delivery of a tin of the precious black sturgeon eggs.

One of my favorite new acquaintances in Washington was Jessica Hobby Catto, a Texas newspaper heiress and dedicated environmentalist with an engaging sense of humor. Her husband, Henry, was a perfect partner. He filled a range of important foreign policy posts, includ- ing ambassador to Great Britain and El Salvador and director of the United States Information Agency. They had friends across the political spectrum, and for all of their achievements the Cattos didn't take themselves too seriously.

When Jessica heard about the caviar deliveries, she made a point, at Ardeshir's next party, of letting the am- bassador know she *adored* caviar.

As she told me later, the next morning when the Ira- nian embassy limousine showed up at their home, she popped the delivered package into the refrigerator, called Henry, and said, "Tonight you'll put on your tux, I'll be in a gown. We'll have a candlelit table and bring out the ambassador's gift."

Henry followed orders, and when all was in place Jes- sica, in her gown, retrieved the embassy package from the refrigerator. The only adornments on the table were delicate china plates, tiny spoons, and a few lemon halves. In great anticipation, Jessica unwrapped the precious package—and broke out laughing.

It was a paperweight with the shah's portrait inside.

To her credit, Jessica told that story everywhere.

Leon Jaworski, a tough Texas lawyer, replaced Archibald Cox as special prosecutor.

CHAPTER 10

FOR PRESIDENT NIXON, the autumn of 1973 was one long political Halloween with a passing parade of hobgoblins, scary surprises, tricks, and very few treats.

He was blindsided by stories about his personal finances, reporting that in 1970 he'd paid only $792.81 in taxes and $878.03 the next year. He decided to take it head-on in an extended appearance before the managing editors of some four hundred of America's newspapers.

To read the complete text now is an instructive experience. He gave his most complete personal explanation yet on Watergate, the Arab oil embargo, and the new special prosecutor, Leon Jaworski, a Democrat from Texas, a former president of the American Bar Association, and a lawyer with a folksy demeanor that masked an unrelenting determination to get what he wanted for his assignment.

The transcript of the editors' session includes nine pages of questions from representatives of large, medium, and smaller newspapers—from *The Washington Post* to the Providence *Evening Bulletin* to the *Democrat and Chronicle* of Rochester, New York. The editors were well prepared with specific questions about two tapes still missing from the cache of nine that had been subpoenaed.

The president blamed an inexpensive recording system (true) and an inconsistent on-off switch for the missing tapes. He wondered aloud how the United States could produce an Apollo space mission to send men to the moon but have such a faulty tape system, at one point saying, "I just wish we'd had a better system," adding, "I frankly wish we hadn't had any system at all, then I wouldn't have to answer this question."

How many times in the autumn of 1973 had that thought crossed his mind?

After Nixon's lengthy defense of the reasons for the missing tapes, Joe Ungaro of the Providence *Evening Bulletin* asked the money question: "You paid $792 in federal income tax in 1970 and $878 in 1971. Are these figures accurate and would you tell us your views on whether elected officials should disclose their personal finances?"

Nixon went into a lengthy defense of his income tax payments and a detailed description of his income over the years when he was a lawyer, not a public servant. Then, in a familiar Nixon turn, he subtly brought someone else into the discussion: his predecessor, Lyndon Johnson. According to Nixon, it was LBJ who'd suggested he could get a substantial tax deduction by donating papers from his years as vice president. In Nixon's words, he turned his papers over to his tax consultants, who had them appraised at half a million dollars, and that valuation was accepted by the IRS. A bit later he went into more detail about his personal finances and unexpectedly gave journalists and the American people a new Nixon phrase for his political lexicon.

He said, "I welcome this kind of examination because people have got to know whether or not their president is a crook."

In a room full of newspaper executives, with the White House press corps listening in, the next day's banner headline was all but set in bold print when the president concluded.

"I'M NOT A CROOK."

One member of the White House press corps who shall go unnamed arrived for breakfast the next morning and feebly tried to explain why he hadn't used that declaration in his lead. (His colleagues just stared into their oatmeal.)

Immediately following his appearance, the president went outside to greet the crowd along the rope line, which was illuminated by bright overhead lights. An Air Force master sergeant was standing with his young son, waiting to greet the president, and Nixon leaned over to say hello to the child. When he stood up, he squinted into the bright lights and asked the sergeant, "Are you the boy's mother or grandmother?"

The startled sergeant said, "Neither."

Nixon took another look and realized his mistake,

saying, "Of course not," and either slapped the man on his cheek or simply patted him affectionately. The word "slap" wound up in some press accounts, and the White House press office went off the rails for the next twenty-four hours. The hullabaloo eventually died down, but even now, after all these years, one of the reporters who wrote "slap" doesn't want to go over the long-ago kerfuffle.

The much larger story, of course, was the "I'm not a crook" declaration following the president's accounting of his personal wealth. Revisiting this part of the Nixon DNA reminded me of earlier stories I'd heard about his obsession with money and personal wealth.

The Quaker poor boy played the common man in public but bought the most expensive estate on the Southern California coast when he became president. He had pricey real estate in Florida. The stories are now common about how he stocked the presidential yacht *Sequoia* with the finest French wines, which stewards wrapped in napkins for the president's personal secret pleasure while his guests were served good but not spectacular California vintages.

Meredith and I were briefly exposed to that side of RN—as he liked to sign his personal messages—while we were still living in California. We were invited to a White House reception. The president's longtime aide and friend Herb Klein, a San Diego newspaperman, spotted us and said, "Tom, the president will be glad to see you. What's new?"

Well, we're building a house on Venice Beach, I said.

Just then we found ourselves in front of Nixon, and Herb relayed our home-building news.

"Venice Beach?" the president said, his eyes lighting up. "What's that going for these days? How much for ocean frontage?"

I stammered something like "Well, ho, ho, it's not cheap," and the president continued: "Is there a lot of building going on there?"

Uh, yes.

It was the first and last time I discussed real estate values with a President.

By the way, that house, a three-story glass-and-cedar custom home overlooking the Pacific, took every saved dime we had or could borrow, $100,000 in 1973. Alas, we couldn't afford to keep it when our East Coast housing needs were elevated.

The beach house long ago shot into the multimillion-dollar range.

*President Nixon's faithful secretary, Rose Mary Woods, re-created
the "stretch" across her desk that the White House used
to try to explain the eighteen and a half minutes
missing from a critical White House tape.*

CHAPTER 11

FOUR DAYS AFTER President Nixon's "I'm not a crook" comment, there was yet another startling development in the Watergate scenario. Fred Buzhardt, the president's White House lawyer, told Judge Sirica that a key White House tape dealing with the scandal had an eighteen-and-a-half-minute gap. The president's faithful executive secretary, Rose Mary Woods, claimed she was responsible; she said that while transcribing the contents of the tape she reached across her desk to answer the telephone and somehow triggered the erase mechanism.

The White House released a photographic re-creation of her stretch, which, rather than fostering widespread confidence in the story, elicited pity that this devoted aide to Nixon had been subjected to such an embarrassing stunt. Later it was revealed that the tape had four stop-and-go erasures, which to many pointed to the president, who had a well-known reputation as a klutz when it came to almost anything that required some degree of mechanical dexterity.

Woods, always faithful, stayed with the president until the very end, when she returned to her childhood home in Ohio, the lingering awkward photograph of her reaching across her desk the enduring legacy of her devotion to Nixon.

The Arab world did not take the loss to Israel during
the Yom Kippur War lightly. Led by Saudi Arabia,
it struck back with a powerful weapon: oil.

CHAPTER 12

WHILE THE PRESIDENT was continuing his feud with the press, he also had political issues that were far more important to the American people. Yes, he had played a major role in saving Israel from a Soviet-Egyptian-Syrian takeover, but the Arab world had not taken the loss lightly. Led by Saudi Arabia, it struck back with a powerful weapon: oil. Oil as a source of gasoline drove so much of America. The United States was shut off from Arab oil exports, and American oil production was dropping.

The Saudi revenge had a devastating effect on the American economy, fueling an acceleration of inflation across the industrial and consumer landscape. We went from a nation of prolific consumers of cheap gas to a nation of frustrated car owners in long lines at service stations, merchants plotting efficient delivery routes, mass transit systems parsing their fuel supplies. Prices for petroleum began to climb steadily. In a year, pump prices for gas went from thirty-eight and a half cents a gallon (hard to believe now) to fifty-five cents a gallon, and that was just the beginning of the progression to where we are now, with gasoline periodically spiking to four dollars plus.

Americans who had seen plentiful, cheap energy as a kind of birthright were suddenly faced with limited supplies at prices ever more dear. What we had taken for granted for so long was gone. Manufacturers and transportation industries were suddenly dealing with a sharp increase in the cost of doing business.

President Nixon launched Project Independence in an effort to rally the country to achieve energy self-reliance. A national speed limit was introduced: fifty-five miles per hour with strict fines, except in the wide-open spaces. This included Montana, where motorists drove fifty-five only when leaving the parking lot and speeding tickets were rare and cost only five dollars to settle.

Kissinger worked to ease the political strains by persuading Israel to withdraw from portions of the Golan Heights and the Sinai following the Yom Kippur War.

By mid-March 1974, the oil embargo was lifted, but while it was underway I had an up-close look at the power of Saudi Arabia's hold on the West as a result of its petroleum holdings.

The Saudi oil minister was a sophisticated member of the royal family named Sheikh Ahmed Zaki Yamani, a dashing prince with a master's from New York University and a Harvard law degree. He was a devoted Muslim and a patron of efforts to preserve his religion and culture. Seemingly overnight he became a household name as he traveled the globe, making the case for the embargo with a soft-spoken lawyer's touch and the petroleum equivalent of holding four aces.

Secretary Kissinger invited the sheikh to a stag dinner at the State Department. It was still the time of the old boys' circuit, and I vividly remember the columnist Rowland Evans grabbing the sheikh on the way in and saying, "When are you bastards gonna let up on us?" Yamani simply smiled and patted Rollie on the arm.

A mix of government, business, and academic leaders sat around a large, horseshoe-shaped table, all watching the soft-spoken sheikh for any sign of concession or willingness to please. This made for a long evening with no payoff.

My dinner partners were George Ball, an aloof and brilliant member of the American diplomatic aristocracy, and Rawleigh Warner, chairman of Mobil Oil. I told Warner that my connection in this crowd was that as a teenager I'd worked for a Mobil gas station one summer. He laughed, and when I saw him on future occasions, he always brought that up.

Although not much was resolved that evening, it was flattering to be included. My self-satisfaction must have shown, for across the table Peter Lisagor fixed me with his crooked grin.

Then he simply broadened the smile and mouthed, "F—— you."

It became a ritual when Peter spotted me in the anchor booth at conventions or being interviewed by local reporters on domestic assignments, his way of deflating any signs of exaggerated self-importance.

Peter's been gone for more than forty years, and I miss him still.

Later I had a slightly different take on Sheikh Yamani when, during an OPEC meeting where the hotel had run out of space, my late colleague Garrick Utley was graciously given a room in the sheikh's enormous suite. Garrick recalled that like any good reporter, he poked around some, and in the sheikh's bedroom he saw a book on the bedside table.

It was the bestseller by pop psychologist Thomas Anthony Harris.

I'm OK—You're OK.

Elaborate schemes to get a tank of gas were the 1970s equivalent of winning the lottery. Unexpectedly, David Brinkley called and in his familiar clipped speaking style asked, "Do you and Meredith like horse racing?"

"Er, sure, I guess so. Why?"

David: "My son works at a gas station and managed to get a full tank of gas. There's a nice little horse track in West Virginia, and I'm driving over. Why don't you and Meredith join Susan and me?"

As we made our way to West Virginia, in the middle of Watergate, the Arab oil embargo, and the deep political division in the country, the horse track promised to be a welcome diversion.

David's presence brought with it the full VIP treatment, including a private box on the finish line with copies of the *Daily Racing Form* opened to the evening's rundown. David, who had reached a pay grade way above mine, was an active player. I knew just enough about the *Racing Form* to win a few and lose a few. Most of all the excursion was a welcome relief from the daily pressure of covering the president and all the complexities of Watergate, which grew more tangled with every passing day.

Nixon was rarely in public. We later learned that beginning in his first term he'd isolate himself late at night with yellow legal pads, scribbling goals to define himself. "Compassionate, Bold, New, Courageous . . . Need to be good to do good . . . Need for joy, serenity, confidence, inspiration."

When the Watergate tapes were made public, the nation heard a different Nixon instructing his chief of staff, Bob Haldeman, to have Richard Helms, director of the CIA, tell the FBI to break off its investigation into Watergate because it was a national security matter. Later the president is heard on tape saying it would not be a problem to get the money to pay off the Watergate burglars to buy their silence.

That and more was yet to come, but a night with the horses and David was a treasured respite.

Nixon and his secretive friend Bebe Rebozo spent a lot of time
together in Key Biscayne, Florida.

CHAPTER 13

I T WAS NOT WIDELY KNOWN that the White House assignment came with a Florida bonus: the president
was a regular in Key Biscayne, Florida, where he spent
many weekends with his friend Bebe Rebozo, the secretive banker whose family was of Cuban descent.

Nixon had gone to Key Biscayne to mull his future
after losing the 1960 presidential election to John F. Kennedy by the slim margin of just over one hundred thousand votes. When Nixon won in 1968, he returned often
to spend time with Rebozo.

Rebozo was single and rarely seen on the social circuit. He had been Nixon's friend since 1950, shortly after
the president was elected to the U.S. Senate from California. Nixon had his own Florida home next door to
Rebozo's property but often stayed with his friend. Rebozo later recalled that the two of them were swimming
when the president got word of the Watergate break-in.

According to Rebozo, the president's first reaction was "What in God's name were they doing there?" Rebozo recalled that they laughed and "forgot about it."

That news received while swimming changed Rebozo's life as well as his friend's. Rebozo's finances were examined, there were unconfirmed stories about their personal relationship, and Rebozo was drawn into the Nixon family's emotional turmoil at the end of the ordeal.

So much of what went on in Key Biscayne was out of reach of the White House press. We endured briefings on routine matters, played tennis, including matches with Haig and Ziegler, and crossed the bridges to Miami Beach to dine at Joe's Stone Crab, the family restaurant that turned the tasty crustacean into a fortune. All these years later I still try to visit Joe's at least once a year to catch up with JoAnn, the granddaughter of the founder, who's become a friend.

While we were busy heading to Joe's or playing tennis, one momentous visit went unappreciated until the president's resignation. As October 1973 gave way to November, Leonard Garment, the president's friend and former law partner, and Fred Buzhardt, the White House counsel, both of whom had reviewed the tapes of the president's meetings with Bob Haldeman and John Dean in which various political and payoff schemes were discussed, realized that the president's claim that he was innocent was demonstrably not true. They had decided to take a bold step and confront the president with their conclusion: he must resign.

They flew to Key Biscayne on the first Saturday in

November and spelled out their case to Haig and Ziegler. It was not just Watergate. There were the other problems: the president had manipulated the donation of his vice presidential papers for a large tax deduction, and he had made that deal with the American dairy industry for richer price supports in exchange for campaign contributions. It was also disclosed that work on his California estate not necessary for security had been done at government expense and had plainly crossed the line.

When they were finished, Haig and Ziegler were stunned.

It would not happen. They insisted that the president would not resign.

The White House press office described the Garment and Buzhardt trip as a routine briefing for the president on legal matters.

Garment and Buzhardt flew back to Washington, and the White House press corps didn't have a clue. So one of the most dramatic developments of Watergate went unreported until Woodward and Bernstein spelled it out in their post-resignation book *The Final Days*.

The Watergate ordeal went on for another nine months.

The White House press corps became a national story during the energy crisis when we were met by the car-rental company that had a contract for our weekend visits. They unloaded on us all the gas guzzlers in their fleet: Cadillacs, big Buicks, Mercury station wagons, and Oldsmobile 98s. I protested, but the rental honcho shrugged and said, "That's all we have." I've always believed that was a cover story. He saw a chance to get top dollar for the fuel hogs no one else wanted.

The Miami press heard about the excesses from outraged local citizens, and we were quickly front-page news, portrayed as elitist consumers who preached parsimony and practiced indulgence.

It was a "gotcha" from the local press. We had it coming.

At Nixon's surprise sixty-first birthday party, his dog,
King Timahoe, enjoyed some cake
off the president's jacket.

CHAPTER 14

A S CHRISTMAS 1973 APPROACHED, Washington was in a suspended state. What would the New Year bring? There were so many loose ends. Members of the House Judiciary Committee were quietly preparing for the possibility of impeachment hearings.

Leon Jaworski, the folksy Texas lawyer with impeccable credentials who had been named special prosecutor after Cox's firing, continued to request material from the White House. Later, during the Ronald Reagan presidency, I found myself on the lower level of the White House with Al Haig, by then Reagan's secretary of state. We were hurrying to a social event on the main floor when he grabbed me and with a sly smile said, "Brokaw, you know this is the Map Room, right?"

Yes, I replied.

"Well," Haig said, "it's too late now to do you any good, but this is where I used to meet Jaworski to argue about the files he wanted."

In 1973, White House reporters didn't get beyond the confines of the press room or the Ziegler operation.

On December 26, 1973, an unexpected call from our Washington news desk. President Nixon and his family were going to California for the holidays but not on *Air Force One*. They had booked much of the first-class cabin of a United Airlines wide-body jet, and they were leaving that evening. It was the president's idea to show the American people that he, too, was making sacrifices during the energy crisis. Never mind that United didn't have the sophisticated communications system or security apparatus fundamental to presidential travel.

Whatever you think of the White House press corps, reporters are also critical components of presidential travel. If something unexpected happens, the public deserves a swift, factual account.

Think back to November 22, 1963, and President Kennedy in Dallas. Merriman Smith of United Press International alerted the world: THREE SHOTS WERE FIRED AT PRESIDENT KENNEDY'S MOTORCADE TODAY IN DOWNTOWN DALLAS. That announcement was followed by another bulletin, this one signaled by a FLASH marker: "Kennedy seriously wounded—perhaps fatally." Smith's eyewitness accounts covered the wounding of Texas governor John Connally and included a quick exchange with a Secret Service agent who said to Smith of the president: "He's dead, Smitty."

Smith continued to file reports from the hospital on the frantic, futile efforts to save the president and then raced to Dallas Love Field, where he filed again before jumping on *Air Force One*, the presidential airliner, with a new mission: to transport Kennedy's body back to Washington with a new president on board: Lyndon B. Johnson.

Smith was already a highly regarded reporter in the small fraternity of Washington wire service reporters. His work that day remains a gold standard for working reporters everywhere.

As a twenty-three-year-old news editor in Omaha, Nebraska, I had read Smith's words on the air after breaking in to a noontime gardening show on KMTV. I distinctly remember thinking, "My God, this doesn't happen in America." It was the end of my prairie naïveté as my career took me through the Sixties, Vietnam, the RFK and Martin Luther King assassinations, the landing on the moon, the rise of China and the fall of the Soviet Union, the 9/11 attack on America, the digital age, and medical miracles.

For President Nixon's December 1973 California trip, the White House did give two reporters advance notice of an hour, but the Secret Service was not happy. The idea of the president flying cross-country in a public airliner with a planeload of civilians who had not been screened was high-risk. And the president's team had also failed to alert the Federal Aviation Administration.

Guess who was running the aviation agency at the time? Alexander Butterfield, the White House staffer who had discovered and disclosed that there was a taping system.

Butterfield, who had a distinguished Air Force career before joining the White House staff, was not pleased by the president's action in flying to California on a commercial flight, or the absence of notification. He said the last-minute disclosure "left precious little time . . . to implement . . . special precautionary procedures which must always be followed" when the president is in the air. Ziegler dismissed the concerns, insisting that the key to the success of the flight was the element of surprise: the White House saw the commercial flight as a PR success, showing the president as a man of the people and setting an example for fuel conservation. "Stunt" was a better description of these arrangements.

The White House press office emphasized that the president had also ordered that no other government aircraft accompany him to the West Coast. No backup plane, no press plane, no courier aircraft or helicopters.

Thankfully, Nixon's daring trip was uneventful, as he sat in the front row of first class in the United airliner.

When I heard about his travel plans, I hurriedly booked a red-eye flight to Los Angeles, determined to file my report from California the next morning on *Today*.

Unfortunately for the Nixon party, the president transported the gloomy Washington atmosphere to the Southern California coastal weather. It was overcast and chilly most of the time we were there, conditions that did give the president real reason to indulge his habit of keeping a wood-burning blaze going in the fireplace, whatever the weather.

Now there was business to be done: finding the president a lawyer skilled in the courtroom if it came to an impeachment trial, one with a reputation for developing a game plan that left nothing to chance.

James St. Clair of Boston, a seasoned courtroom litigator, native of Ohio, got the call. When he arrived in California, he was slipped into La Casa Pacifica for his first meeting with the president. As Woodward and Bernstein reported later, Nixon emphasized that he wanted St. Clair to represent the office of the presidency, not the man. At the end of their one-hour meeting, St. Clair was ushered out to meet with Al Haig, who closed the deal: $42,500 a year for salary, with support staff to be settled later.

St. Clair was familiar with high-profile Washington cases. As a young lawyer he had been at the side of another Boston lawyer, Joe Welch, for one of the enduring moments in capital lore. It was Welch who famously said to the infamous Senator Joe McCarthy, after one of McCarthy's rants on Communist influence on the Army, "Have you no sense of decency, sir? At long last, have you left no sense of decency?" It was the defining moment in the Senate hearing on McCarthy. McCarthy's poisonous public notoriety faded quickly. For young James St. Clair, it was a memory he later shared with his new staff representing Nixon.

That gloomy December, California was hardly a festive getaway location. The Arab oil embargo was still on, one of the president's daughters had stayed in the East, and the newspapers were preparing their year-end reviews, which would be heavy on Watergate and projections about what would be likely to happen to Nixon.

California remained cold and rainy throughout the president's stay, so his clerical staff decided he needed cheering up on his sixty-first birthday, in early January. They arranged a "surprise" cake for La Casa Pacifica and rounded up a press pool to cover the festivities. Helen Thomas grumbled as she boarded the bus for the ride to the seaside mansion, filling her role as a pool reporter.

When the bus returned, Helen was first off and laughing so hard we could barely understand her, but once the videotape of the "party" rolled, we all were convulsed.

The opening scene is outside the president's office, where a large frosted cake is on a wheeled table. When the doors to the office swing open, we can see the president in a dark blazer and tie as the staff sings out, "Happy Birthday, Mr. President!" while wheeling the cake up to his desk.

The president is obviously pleased as he gets up from the desk, leaning over the cake to blow out the candles. In a Nixonian move he leans too far, and when he stands up his jacket is covered with white frosting. King Timahoe, his handsome Irish setter, knows a good deal when he sees one and races over to lick the frosting off his master's jacket.

As the staff frantically yells, "Cut the cameras! No more pictures," the president tilts the cake so Timahoe can have a long, slurping taste.

Finally the cameras are shut off, but the embarrassing moment has been caught on tape.

The cake fiasco was a fitting harbinger of what was to come in the new year.

After a few days Meredith joined me in Orange County and got a close-up look at the life of a network correspondent even when the news was thin. The daily effort to get material on *Nightly News* was a frenetic exercise in cars, motorcycles, and helicopters.

This was well before the digital age, so I would race to a nearby helicopter launchpad by two o'clock California time to catch a thirty-minute flight to NBC in Burbank; there I'd write and edit that night's story for *NBC Nightly News,* anchored by John Chancellor, and maybe leave something behind for the next morning's *Today* show. Then back on the chopper for the return to San Clemente.

With so little meaningful news out of the White House, dinner plans were always a high priority. Meredith and I had a long-standing favorite: Matteo's, a popular Italian restaurant connected to its glittering cousin of the same name in West Los Angeles. That the original Matteo's was owned by a Hoboken boyhood friend of Frank Sinatra's made it a regular watering hole for big-name Hollywood stars.

When we had first arrived in Los Angeles, friends suggested meeting at Matteo's on Westwood after a football game. There, Willie, the bartender, wondered where we were from. When we said South Dakota, his eyes widened and he asked Matty, the owner, "Do we fly over South Dakota when we come from Hoboken?" Then he commented on Meredith's youthful beauty and asked a rugged guy with his back turned if he agreed.

It was Lee Marvin, and he endorsed Willie's assessment.

It was the beginning of a familial relationship with Matty and the Hoboken crowd. We felt like favorite offspring.

When the Orange County Matteo's opened, we were

seated in a booth next to a familiar figure who had been driven up from San Clemente: Henry Kissinger. He was with a striking White House staffer not yet well known but destined for her own fame: Diane Sawyer.

For his part, the president remained holed up in La Casa Pacifica except for the occasional solitary walk along the Pacific. As one of my colleagues put it, "The president left D.C. but brought his cloud with him."

PART II

1974

*Nixon's 1974 State of the Union address was the only one
to feature Gerald Ford in the vice president's seat.*

CHAPTER 15

A T THE END OF HIS CALIFORNIA STAY, the president
went back to the fleet of *Air Force One*, with the
usual backup staff carriers, military escorts, and the attendant bells and whistles for the commander in chief.
He returned to Washington with his new lawyer and
plans for taking on Watergate in his State of the Union
address. But first his new vice president, Gerald Ford,
landed on the network news and on front pages with an
appearance on *Meet the Press*.

I asked Mr. Ford if he agreed with the president's decision not to release presidential documents to the Senate Watergate Committee, which was still investigating
White House behavior connected to the burglaries. The
vice president initially agreed, saying the request for five
hundred documents was a scattergun approach.

But wouldn't the current environment be better
served by a compromise agreement? Mr. Ford called the

request a "fishing expedition" and then went off message, saying, "I hope and trust that as we go down the road perhaps there can be some compromise."

As I pressed on, the vice president again strayed from the White House line, saying that if there were some refinements in the Senate Committee's request for documents, there might in fact be room for compromise. You could almost hear the White House expletives from Pennsylvania Avenue all the way to the outer fringes of the District.

The next day the White House indicated that the vice president had been speaking "on his own" and that nothing had changed since the president's refusal to hand over the subpoenaed tape documents.

Meanwhile, the president kept preparing for the State of the Union address before a joint session of Congress and a vast television audience.

Personal images from the night of that address—January 30, 1974—remain. As a pool reporter, I joined the dramatic caravan of the presidential limousine, Secret Service vehicles, and motorcycle escorts racing through the dark from the White House to Capitol Hill. We traveled at high speed along Pennsylvania Avenue, where just the year before the president had paraded in the triumphant glory of his reelection. Now the country faced an uncertain future as the president arrived to make his case again as chief executive beyond the reach of Congress.

Inside the Capitol Building, an air of courtesy mixed with curiosity about what the president would say.

He opened with the standard good news, bad news

assessment: "We meet here tonight at a time of great challenges and great opportunities for America." He expressed hope that America's longest war—Vietnam— would be followed by America's longest peace. That received a rousing reception. He then introduced "a personal word with regard to"—and here his tone took on a dismissive note—"the so-called Watergate affair."

The president challenged his adversaries: "I believe the time has come to bring that investigation and the other investigations of this matter to an end.

"One year of Watergate is enough!"

That challenge brought a booming round of applause from the Republican side of the House chamber. It was also a preview of the president's strategy, so familiar to his political opponents. The best defense for Nixon was always a strong offense. And we would quickly learn that he intended to use the symbolic and real power of his office at every turn. One could imagine him saying to himself late at night with his yellow legal pad in his lap as he sat in a favorite easy chair, "You are the president, goddammit—act like it."

The New Year was to be a stage for Nixon to deal anew with the Soviet Union, the Middle East, and domestic initiatives; his presence would be required at natural disasters and ceremonial events, where his office added to the grandeur. But that was the stage. The reality was contained in the tape recordings stored in the White House, the tapes with the president's own voice clearly showing he was an active participant in the Watergate cover-up. Those were the separate worlds of Richard Nixon as he headed into what would be his final months in office.

There was no more telling sign of Nixon's depleted influence than in the "thumb" of eastern Michigan, near Gerald Ford's congressional district, which had been safe territory for Republicans since early in the twentieth century. Despite pleas from Michigan Republicans to stay in Washington, Nixon invaded Vice President Ford's neighborhood for a dreary day of campaigning, with sparse crowds and a funereal atmosphere. When a special election was held to fill a reliably Republican House seat in Ford's home state, the Democratic candidate won comfortably, the first loss for Republicans in that district in forty-two years.

*The president's attorney, James St. Clair (left),
conferring with John Doar, lead counsel for
the House Judiciary Committee.*

CHAPTER 16

OLLOWING THE PRESIDENT'S State of the Union address, there was no indication on Capitol Hill, in the federal judiciary, or in the national news media that Watergate had a calendar end date. Too many questions remained for it to be closed down simply because a year had passed.

Special prosecutor Leon Jaworski was a formidable adversary as he demanded White House files and transcripts of tape recordings. A federal grand jury also remained in session, and on the Hill, House Democrats were preparing for the possibility of impeachment proceedings. So the president was surrounded by investigators. Woodward and Bernstein were now joined by other journalists from around the world on what had become a global fascination: Would the president of the United States be brought down?

For his part, Nixon was dealing with a tightly controlled group of advisers: Haig; the lawyer St. Clair; White House counsel Buzhardt, who we now know thought the president was guilty; Ziegler, now expanding his role as a political adviser as well as a militant defender of the president; Pat Buchanan, the commando with a speechwriter's lance.

On the Democratic side, a little-known New Jersey Congressman, Peter Rodino, was chairman of the House Judiciary Committee, and he had selected a Republican lawyer with impeccable credentials to be the lead counsel for his committee's investigation of Watergate. John Doar was a fifty-two-year-old Wisconsin Republican who had earned a sterling reputation in the 1960s. Doar had headed the Civil Rights Division of Justice during the Kennedy administration, and he had bravely waded into violent demonstrations organized by angry white crowds, appealing for calm. He brought the same quiet courage and measured deportment to his new job as chief counsel of House Judiciary. His party registration as a Republican was a big plus.

At the end of February, we were aware that the federal grand jury that had been hearing evidence on Watergate for twenty-one months was ready to report. Special prosecutor Jaworski met with the jurors and found a fired-up crowd. They wanted to indict Richard Nixon as well as Haldeman, Ehrlichman, former attorney general John Mitchell, Chuck Colson, and other Nixon acolytes involved in the illegal activities. Jaworski was sympathetic, but he persuaded the jury that there was a better way to hold the president accountable: impeachment. They withheld news of the most explosive codicil in their verdict: Richard Nixon was an unindicted co-conspirator. It leaked out a couple of months later, and I can still see Helen Thomas parading through the White House press room, waving the press account and saying over and over again, "Nixon is an unindicted co-conspirator."

The president would not stand trial in a federal courtroom, but with impeachment proceedings advancing, his role as judged by a citizen jury was clear. It was difficult for even the most faithful followers of the president to dismiss that reality.

Once a month I'd slip out of the White House and head to Capitol Hill to measure the attitudes of two senators who were in leadership positions but were not firebrands: Robert Byrd of West Virginia, the canny senior Democratic senator, and Robert Griffin of Michigan, the number two Republican in the Senate.

When the grand jury's "unindicted co-conspirator" judgment was released, Senator Griffin's implacable expression and extra-cautious comments changed. He acknowledged that it was a serious blow but, ever circumspect, reminded me that the assessment had come from a District of Columbia grand jury. Nonetheless, he deliberately chose not to defend the president to me. That was a shift.

In Griffin's outer office, visitors could pick up a copy of Mrs. Griffin's cookbook featuring recipes made with Michigan apples. In Senator Byrd's office, the public pamphlets for visiting West Virginia constituents were instructions on the most efficient way to castrate a hog.

Byrd sat at a table covered with those instructions

and gave me a lesson in the most efficient way to deal with a reporter. Always a man of the people and a senator with a reputation for deal making, Byrd would invariably open our conversations by asking, "What are they up to now down at the White House?" I'd remind him that I was there to plumb *his* thinking on how Democrats were planning to go forward.

Impeachment was a House of Representatives responsibility, but the Democratic Party beyond the House had skin in this game. Up until the grand jury report, Byrd had been very cautious; now he acknowledged that the grand jury's co-conspirator verdict made it easier for Democrats in both chambers to move forward more aggressively.

On the way out of his office, I grabbed one of the hog castration pamphlets because, well, you never know.

Dan Rather asking Nixon a question at the National Association of Broadcasters. My question was the last one of the night—and the last question of any press conference President Nixon would hold.

CHAPTER 17

WHEN MARCH 1974 ARRIVED, the pace of the Watergate developments and the case against the president accelerated. The month opened with the grand jury indictments against seven principal aides to the president: John Mitchell, his former attorney general; a campaign aide, Robert Mardian; Bob Haldeman, his former chief of staff; former domestic affairs chief John Ehrlichman; Charles Colson, former White House counsel; Kenneth Parkinson, attorney for the 1972 reelection committee; and Gordan Strachan, a former aide to Haldeman. It was this grand jury report that also included Richard Nixon as an unindicted co-conspirator.

That same month Robert Redford's film company paid $450,000 for the film rights to Woodward and Bernstein's yet-to-be-published *All the President's Men*. It would have been a bargain at twice the price, given the film's subsequent financial and cultural success.

George Shultz, the highly regarded GOP establishment figure, a former World War II Marine and a professor of economics, quietly resigned as secretary of the
treasury.

As for the president, he continued what had become
his road tour in an effort to demonstrate that he was
doing business as usual, even with the threat of impeachment growing more likely every week. He was to
address the National Association of Broadcasters in
Houston, Texas, in mid-March and take questions from
a mix of local broadcast journalists and some of us from
the White House press corps.

For some time I had been harboring a question about
the limits of executive privilege. Specifically, I wanted to
know if executive privilege applied in impeachment
proceedings—an ever more important question as the
prospects of an impeachment trial seemed more likely.
My research assistant had canvassed prominent constitutional scholars, and the consensus was that executive
privilege was not applicable in impeachment trials.
Given the president's assertion that executive privilege
was viable even in impeachment cases, I understood
that we were on new ground. However, before I could
ask my question, the moderator called Dan Rather to
the microphone.

Houston was Dan's hometown, and when he introduced himself—"Dan Rather of CBS News"—he drew a
hearty round of applause, with some boos in the mix.
The president responded in a way that was interpreted
as hostile by some and just a little edgy by others.

"Are you running for something, Mr. Rather?"

Dan shot back, "No sir, Mr. President. Are you?"

There was a short collective inhalation by the audience and then a mix of laughter and boos.

After a preamble, this was Dan's question: "How can the House meet its constitutional responsibilities while you, the person under investigation, are allowed to limit their access to potential evidence?"

The president responded that the special prosecutor, Leon Jaworski, had indicated that he had all he needed on the Watergate story. Dan followed up with a repeat of his initial question: If the House of Representatives has the constitutional authority to investigate, how can the president limit that authority? Nixon said, essentially, that if the House would adhere to its limits as spelled out in the Constitution, then he would as well.

It was the perfect setup for my question.

"Mr. President, Tom Brokaw of NBC News, following on my colleague Dan Rather's question.

"You have referred here again tonight, as you have in the past, about what you call the precedents of past presidents in withholding White House material from the House Judiciary Committee.

"But other presidents protecting the confidentiality of their conversations were not the subject of impeachment investigations, Mr. President, and in fact many of them wrote that the House Judiciary Committee . . . had the right to demand White House materials in the course of the impeachment investigations. And history shows that Andrew Johnson gave up everything that the Congress asked him for when he was the subject of an impeachment investigation.

"So, Mr. President, my question is this: Aren't your statements historically inaccurate or at least misleading?"

The president conceded that the description of Andrew Johnson was correct, but he quickly reverted to his position that the principle of presidential confidentiality still stands, *even in cases of impeachment.* I knew from our research and from conversations with legal scholars, such as Alexander Bickel, a conservative professor at Yale Law School, that impeachment proceedings were exempt from claims of executive privilege.

The next day Ron Ziegler upbraided me for challenging the president's interpretation, suggesting that it was the chief executive's prerogative to interpret the law, not mine.

At dinner later that night in Houston, most of the buzz was about the Nixon-Rather confrontation. Should Dan have resisted the exchange? Adam Clymer, the acerbic correspondent for the Baltimore *Sun* and later for *The New York Times,* volunteered, "Very funny, Mr. President. Why don't you tell us: Were you responsible for the eighteen-and-a-half-minute gap in the Watergate tape."

We all gave Adam high fives, but then he came clean.

"Of course," he said, "it took me two hours to think of that, and I wasn't on television."

Self-deprecation is a virtue rarely exhibited in the White House press corps.

Nixon at Notre-Dame for the memorial service for
President Georges Pompidou of France.

CHAPTER 18

DESPITE NIXON'S CLAIM that one year of Watergate was enough, the grand jury, which had declared him an "unindicted co-conspirator," sent to the House Judiciary Committee its report that the president was an active participant in the cover-up. The Judiciary legal team, in turn, took the report to Judge Sirica, the U.S. district judge who presided over the Watergate cases, for a two-hour review. So we had two scenarios operating simultaneously: the president adopting publicly, again, a "What, me worry?" attitude and the House Judiciary Committee pressing ahead, collecting material that would justify impeachment proceedings. We now know, thanks to the post-resignation reporting of Bob Woodward and Carl Bernstein, that the president's legal and senior political team was struggling to find a plausible exit for the president from his trail of incriminating behavior.

As for Nixon, any excuse to get out of town and be the president was welcome. In early April he found an ideal opportunity.

The president of France, Georges Pompidou, who had a rare blood cancer, died at the age of sixty-two. Pompidou was originally an acolyte of Charles de Gaulle's but had established his own distinctive legacy as prime minister by improving relations with the United States while strengthening the French economy. He served a record six years as prime minister before becoming president, and so his funeral was a grand affair.

As the pool reporter for the White House press— lucky me—I had a close-up view of the proceedings, including Nixon's determination to make the most of any public opportunities. Although it was a time of mourning in France, Nixon immediately took to the streets of Paris, working the friendly crowds around the majestic American embassy as if he didn't have a care in the world.

One enthusiastic bystander shouted out, "Mr. President! I'm from Ohio. I'm an American!" The president looked at the man with an expression of pure delight, responding in his awkward way, "You're an American? So am I!" It was not a joke. It was one more example of Nixon's earnest but baffling attempt to make small talk.

The American embassy was soon awash with long limousines as Nixon set up shop for meetings with the leaders of Italy, West Germany, Great Britain, Denmark, Japan, and the Soviet Union. The French were not happy with this American trying to hang on to his job by exploiting their mourning for his own purposes.

At Notre-Dame Cathedral, the roped-off area for the press offered only a limited view of the state funeral proceedings. Providentially, a friendly young priest who spoke English motioned for me to follow him to a worn wooden door behind the majestic altar area. It opened to a steep staircase weathered by time. Nan Robertson of *The New York Times* and I hiked straight up into the upper reaches of the cathedral, expecting to meet Quasimodo at every turn.

Finally, we reached another worn door and opened it to find ourselves on a narrow balcony at the highest reaches of the twelfth-century cathedral. It provided a sweeping view of the altar, the pews filled with presidents and kings, queens and grandes dames, military strongmen and families with wealth beyond the hopes of small republics from what was then called the Third World. The shah of Iran stood in the front pew alongside Haile Selassie, the diminutive emperor of Ethiopia. And there on the left side of the first pew was Richard Nixon, the president of the United States, making full use of the title that had brought him to this moment of grandeur and mourning for a distinguished statesman.

What could he have been thinking about his own farewell, or even about what awaited him once the Paris weekend was over?

The president would spend the night in Paris, and then a presidential limousine would take him to *Air Force One,* and that distinctive 707 would head back across the Atlantic to the reality of Watergate, which was growing more contentious with every passing day.

While he was away, his faithful appointments secretary, Dwight Chapin, another of the Southern California troupe, was found guilty of two counts of lying to the Watergate grand jury. The pace toward impeachment was quickening, but Nixon was already planning more trips that would allow him to be president and not an unindicted co-conspirator.

William Cohen, then a freshman member of Congress from Maine, proved himself to be a maverick early on.

CHAPTER 19

WHILE NIXON WAS WORKING HARD during his Paris stay to demonstrate that his power as America's commander in chief was undiminished, there was a different reality in Washington.

One of those awaiting the president's return was a freshman Republican congressman from Maine, William Cohen, the son of a Jewish father and a Christian mother; he was my age during the summer that would change his life. He arrived in the capital with a law degree, an interest in poetry, a reputation back home as a high school basketball star, and a history of success in local politics. Another freshman representative on the House Judiciary Committee was a fiery Democrat, Liz Holtzman of New York, but Cohen attracted more attention because he didn't fit the conventional GOP model. He quickly drew notice as an independent voice.

We met as a result of a mutual friendship with Pete

Dawkins, the West Point Heisman Trophy winner, Rhodes scholar, and Vietnam veteran. Bill had already achieved a measure of notoriety during a House Judiciary Committee hearing on Gerald Ford's ascension to the vice presidency.

Ford had been the GOP leader in the House, so the questions from his former colleagues were collegial. When Cohen's turn came, he referred to recent stories that the White House had attempted to recruit a federal judge to head the FBI while the judge was presiding over the trial of Daniel Ellsberg for leaking the Pentagon Papers. Ford dismissed the concerns by saying simply that it was bad judgment and then drew laughter from his fellow Republicans by remarking that the FBI job would be a demotion.

Cohen, the new kid on that side of the aisle, was not amused. The next day he emphasized the gravity of the attempt to compromise the judge who was presiding in the Ellsberg trial, a trial of great importance. The freshman GOP congressman told the next vice president of the United States that this blatant interference in the Ellsberg trial was a gross violation of due process. Cohen wound up his time by praising Ford's past record on the rule of law and, in an adroit turn, said he was confident that the incoming vice president would uphold the highest standards.

His Republican elders on the House Judiciary Committee were not pleased. The rookie had taken on the party member who could very well become the next president. Cohen was immediately labeled a maverick in his party, a brash upstart. Past contributors to his campaign wrote and called his office, saying in no uncertain terms, *You have betrayed your party; expect no help from me.* Nonetheless, when the House Judiciary Committee moved deeper into the impeachment proceedings, Cohen continued to defy his party's expectations and voted with Chairman Peter Rodino on key questions about whether to proceed with impeachment.

In the end, Cohen was right and he was rewarded with recognition by *Time* magazine as one of America's 200 Future Leaders. He also was named by the national Junior Chamber of Commerce as one of the Ten Outstanding Young Men in America. He went on to win three terms as a U.S. senator from Maine, but because of his independence he was rarely mentioned as a standard-bearer for the GOP.

Cohen became so frustrated with the rigid partisanship that he decided to leave politics after a total of three three terms in the House and three in the Senate, but Bill Clinton intervened, nominating Cohen successfully for secretary of defense in 1997, a good fit for his broad experience in national security and international political matters.

Watergate changed a lot of lives, not many of them for the better, but Bill Cohen was an exception. While other young men his age were going off to jail, he was making his mark with his Maine independence.

*The destruction from the Xenia, Ohio, tornado
was devastating, and unlike anything President Nixon
had ever before witnessed.*

CHAPTER 20

PRESIDENT NIXON IN THE SPRING OF 1974 was on the lookout for any opportunity to be an empathetic commander in chief. In early April a rash of devastating tornadoes—some of the most destructive ever—swept across the South and the Midwest, leveling everything in their paths. One bore down on Xenia, Ohio, a prosperous small city in the southwestern part of the state, founded in 1803 and later well known for a large orphanage established to care for children who had lost parents in the Civil War.

Early one morning, the phone rang in our home on Woodley Road, announcing a call from the White House: *The president is going to Xenia. You're the broadcast pool reporter.*

As a child of the Great Plains, I was a tornado veteran, but Xenia was shocking. The town took a direct hit, and the twister, one of 148 that day, leveled vast swaths of residential neighborhoods, commercial districts, and public areas. Thirty-four people were killed.

When Nixon arrived, there was none of the usual commotion accompanying a presidential visit. The extent of the damage created a kind of vacuum; there was an eerie stillness as residents and first responders picked through the damage.

The president appeared to be shocked as well, saying several times, "Just total devastation, this is the worst I have seen." He promised immediate federal disaster relief, and then the president moved on to the town square to confer with local officeholders.

As he stood in a huddle of relief workers and city officials, a woman approached along a sidewalk across the street. She stopped and said aloud in the quiet of the moment, "Is that Nixon? Impeach him! Impeach him!" Her voice was like a fire alarm going off. A Secret Service agent moved to quiet her, but it was too late. The president didn't turn, although his shoulders tightened, and when his aide Steve Bull directed him toward the city hall, the president rejected his help, saying, "I know where I am going!"

Two footnotes to that day: when Xenia was founded, the city fathers gave it that Greek name because it means "hospitality" and "friendship." Xenia was also the boyhood stomping grounds of Arthur Schlesinger, Jr., the renowned American historian. His grandfather had emigrated there from Europe. Schlesinger was well known not only as a writer and historian but also as a close family friend of the Kennedys and a persistent critic of Nixon, the man and the politician.

President Nixon made a show of releasing edited transcripts of many Watergate tapes. America was introduced to the term "expletive deleted."

CHAPTER 21

TRY AS NIXON MIGHT to separate himself from Watergate, the scandal continued to be an unrelenting presence. As the House Judiciary Committee and special prosecutor Jaworski continued to build their case, the White House team knew it would have to make *some* effort to slow the momentum. The House Judiciary Committee had issued a subpoena for forty-two White House conversations and Jaworski had issued a subpoena for material related to sixty-four White House conversations.

In late April 1974, the president went on national television to announce that he would make public transcriptions from more than forty-two White House conversations related to Watergate in response to the House Judiciary subpoena. He explained that he had theretofore refused to do so because some of the transcripts contained state secrets protected by executive privilege.

In his most earnest fashion, he explained he had edited the tapes to exclude material "not relevant" to the Watergate investigation. The transcripts were in expensive binders stacked behind the president, in full view of the cameras. The visuals gave the impression that there were maybe a thousand pages in each binder, when in fact heavy editing had reduced the number of pages to a much more modest amount. The next day the show continued in full view of our cameras, as binders were loaded into the back of a White House station wagon parked in the circular driveway at the West Wing, to be driven to Capitol Hill.

The most damaging transcripts were held until late in the afternoon to make it more difficult for the press to review the contents and get the relevant parts onto the 6:30 news shows and into the next day's newspapers.

After working late into the evening to prepare reports for the *Today* show, I returned home well after dinner to a plate of fried chicken Meredith had left out.

She came downstairs to find me standing in the kitchen with a transcript in one hand and a chicken leg in the other, transfixed by reading Oval Office conversations that were stunningly candid and crude. The president had said that getting a million dollars in cash for payoffs would not be easy, "but it could be done."

The decision to release the tapes was an indication of just how delusional the president and his team had become. Leading Republicans on Capitol Hill were stunned by much of what they were reading.

In an exchange with John Dean, the president volunteered that "maybe it takes a gang to do that," to manage the money. Mind you, these were the least damaging conversations, in the eyes of the White House. America was hereby introduced to the term "expletive deleted."

Many years later, while I was organizing material from my White House days, the thick blue book containing the transcripts of the White House tapes turned up with a dark stain on the cover.

The last of the chicken leg.

Ron Ziegler, Bob Haldeman's protégé as an ad man,
became one of Nixon's top advisers as chief
of communications. Ziegler stayed
with Nixon until the end.

CHAPTER 22

RELATIONSHIPS BETWEEN the White House senior staff and the correspondents were not as testy as they are in the age of Trump—we'd occasionally share a drink or a tennis match—but the tension was always present. One day during the time the House Judiciary Committee was gearing up for impeachment hearings, Ron Ziegler called.

"Lemme buy you lunch," he said in that gravelly voice, and the tone didn't seem cordial.

We took a booth at Sans Souci, the power brokers' hangout around the corner from the White House. He ordered a Rob Roy and veal piccata and got right to his message: "You're a disappointment, Tom. We thought you'd come to the White House with a fresh attitude, but you've jumped right in with the Georgetown crowd."

"Ron," I said, "first, that's an overstatement, and second, I don't think I ordered up the impeachment proceedings which are now under way."

We were still sparring in that tone a few minutes later when suddenly Paul, the maître d', dropped a note on our table. Ziegler got to it before I did, read it, flipped it to me, and said, "I rest my case." And then, to his credit, he laughed.

The note said,

Hey, kid, I guess this means you're not coming to Hickory Hill for dinner tonight.

Love, Ethel

Ethel Kennedy was sitting at a table across the room, and although I had *not* been invited to dinner, she knew a great joke opportunity when she saw it. The Ethel intervention defused the tension, and Ron and I had a leisurely walk back to the White House.

*President Nixon visited friendly territory at a
campaign-like rally in Phoenix.*

CHAPTER 23

B Y MAY 1974, PRESIDENT NIXON had decided that his best hope was to get out of Washington and revert to a campaign mode. Senator Barry Goldwater, who was increasingly concerned about the president's state of mind, agreed to stage a campaign-like rally for him in Phoenix on May 3.

Goldwater, along with Arizona congressman John Rhodes, the House minority leader, and Arizona governor Jack Williams, gave the president a five-star welcome, praising him as a "great president" to an enthusiastic audience, estimated at fifteen thousand, in Phoenix's Veterans Memorial Coliseum. Goldwater told reporters, "I believe the American people aren't worried about" Watergate.

A noisy crowd of anti-Nixon protestors had congregated outside the coliseum, but the evening belonged to the Nixon enthusiasts. Those of us in the White House press corps were huddled on the floor of the auditorium feeling like members of a hostage collective as Nixon supporters screamed at us, "Traitors! Liars!"

The president, warmed by the enthusiastic reception, was in full campaign mode, saying again, "I believe the time has come to put Watergate behind us and get on with the business of America!"

The president and Mrs. Nixon went from the rally to a private party at the home of Senator Goldwater, where they must have been grateful for the distance between Arizona and Washington, D.C. By all appearances, it had been a successful event, and now they would continue on to Spokane, Washington, and the opening of a world's fair with an environmental theme.

When Fred Zimmerman and I settled into our seats on the charter flight, an eager young flight attendant came over to share her excitement about seeing the president at the next stop. Fred looked up and said in his droll manner, "He's going to f——— it up." Unnerved, the attendant retreated to her station in the galley.

I turned to Fred and exclaimed, "Why did you say that?" Fred answered wearily, "Hey, he got the last appearance right. He never gets two in a row right."

When we arrived in Spokane, Fred invited the young woman to join us, explaining that we could get her inside the rope line. The host on the stage was Washington governor Dan Evans, a popular moderate Republican, tall, handsome, and distinguished. He was also a close friend of William Ruckelshaus, a fellow resident of Washington State who had resigned his Department of Justice position during the Saturday Night Massacre.

Nixon was plainly uncomfortable standing next to Governor Evans, who was known to be critical of him. Evans stepped up to the microphone and used an appropriate but minimal introduction for a chief executive: "It is my high honor and personal privilege to introduce the president of the United States." No additional flourishes.

Nixon, who was on this trip to put Watergate behind us, stepped to the microphone and said, "Uh, thank you, thank you, Governor Evidence.

"I mean Evans!"

Fred turned to the flight attendant and said, "See, I told you . . ."

Twenty-five years later I encountered Governor Evans at a University of Washington commencement ceremony and said, "Governor, I was in Spokane—" and before I could finish he laughed and said, "Governor *Evidence*, right?"

Wearing the cloak of the presidency, President Nixon got a pharaoh's welcome in Egypt as millions lined the route.

CHAPTER 24

RICHARD NIXON'S CAMPAIGN-LIKE STOPS didn't keep the world from closing in on him later in May 1974.

The *Chicago Tribune* had long been considered a bulwark of conservative journalism. (This was the newspaper so eager to see Harry Truman defeated in his run for president in 1948 that it went to press early and mistakenly with the headline DEWEY DEFEATS TRUMAN—a copy of which was held aloft by a smiling Harry Truman.) In early May, this venerable voice of midwestern conservatism urged Nixon to leave office for the good of "the Presidency, the country, and the free world."

In the same month it was disclosed that in 1971, top leaders in the dairy industry had tried to raise $300,000 for the president shortly after he agreed to support a rise in milk prices. On May 15 his faithful former appointments secretary, Dwight Chapin, was sentenced to ten months in prison for lying to a Watergate grand jury.

Jeb Magruder, a collegiate tennis star and successful businessman before he moved to California and got involved in GOP politics, was sentenced to a prison term of ten months to four years for his role in organizing the Watergate break-in. When he was released from prison, Magruder would become an ordained minister and at one point implicate President Nixon as an active organizer of the break-in. However, in later articles he would back off from placing Nixon in the original plans.

Also in May, Richard Kleindienst, the former attorney general, pleaded guilty to a misdemeanor for lying in an antitrust case.

For his part, Nixon stuck to his strategy of wearing the cloak of the presidency wherever he went. He planned two epic trips, one to the Middle East and one to the Soviet Union, to prove he was still a working president.

*During a visit to the Soviet Union, President Nixon hoped
for a breakthrough on nukes with Russian leader
Leonid Brezhnev at the resort town of Oreanda.*

CHAPTER 25

THE MIDDLE EASTERN TRIP became an extravagant showcase for Nixon, but it did him little good. He made a high-profile entry in Egypt for meetings with Egyptian president Anwar Sadat, but the news from home was bleak. For the first time, a majority of the American people in the latest Harris Poll favored his impeachment and removal from office.

In Egypt, Nixon was receiving a welcome fit for a pharaoh. However, he had developed and kept secret a severe case of phlebitis, a dangerous and uncomfortable clot in his calf. If it had broken loose and raced to his heart, it could have killed him.

Nonetheless, he pushed on. On a slow train ride to Alexandria from Cairo, Nixon and Egyptian president Sadat might as well have been sun kings from Egypt's golden age. Millions of people lined the route, many of them openly expressing their gratitude for Nixon's role as a peacemaker in the war with Israel. Ironically, that role had involved giving Israel the military means to defeat Egypt and bring the war to a halt. One more example of the enigmatic, often baffling way of the Middle East.

After stops in Tel Aviv, Jordan, and Syria, the president turned for home energized by his receptions in the Middle East, but there were no adoring crowds lining his route to the White House. His standing in national polls continued to sink as the House Judiciary Committee was moving steadily toward formal impeachment hearings.

One of our Woodley Road neighbors, Paul Nitze, the quintessential intellectual public servant—wealthy, highly educated, and fiercely private—announced that he was resigning from the Strategic Arms Limitation Talks with the Soviet Union because of what he called the depressing reality of Watergate, which made the prospects of slowing the arms race unlikely.

But the president was already packing his bags for another international trip, this one to Moscow, where he hoped to strike a new arms control deal with Leonid Brezhnev, who, the year before, had seemed open to the idea. However, Nitze's pessimistic analysis would soon come to define the new round of talks.

As the president prepared to leave for Moscow, one of his favorite political hit men, Charles Colson, was sentenced for his role in organizing dirty tricks out of his White House office. He had been Nixon's favorite "tough guy" during the 1972 campaign, but when he was caught deliberately trying to destroy Daniel Ellsberg's reputation, Colson was sentenced to prison; there he had a spiritual rebirth as a Christian evangelist, concentrating on prison inmates.

Colson devoted the rest of his life to criminal justice reform with a Christian underpinning. It was by all accounts a genuine conversion and a worthy cause. Colson had a lot to atone for. He was an all-purpose hatchet man who compiled the White House "enemies list," a collection of journalists, politicians, and activists he thought of as threats to the Nixon presidency. He zeroed in on Daniel Ellsberg, a former Marine who as a Pentagon planner put together a devastating critique of the Vietnam War—and leaked it to *The New York Times* and *The Washington Post*. Colson orchestrated a campaign to discredit Ellsberg and was eventually convicted of obstruction of justice. Colson's prison experience led him to a religious awakening and he spent the rest of his life as a spiritual counselor and advocate for the underclass. So as the president departed for what he hoped would be a triumphant trip to Moscow, his favorite hatchet man was reporting for his life-changing stint in prison.

The president had high hopes for a new nuclear arms reduction that would demonstrate his powers as an indispensable international statesman, but while his party was en route to Moscow, Secretary Kissinger warned him that the signals on that count were not encouraging. Nonetheless, Soviet general secretary Leonid Brezhnev treated the president as an old friend, praising his help in improving economic relations between the two countries.

For those of us making our first visits to Moscow, it

was a head-shaking experience. The ancient capital was a dreary, joyless city with a permanent overlay of foul air and cheerless citizens hurrying through the streets with their heads down. When I stepped into Red Square to do a report for our cameras, a young man paused to watch and was immediately sent away by a burly traffic cop waving a menacing wood baton.

The Intourist Hotel for visiting foreigners was more like a worn army barracks with cheap beds and thin blankets. A house mother was stationed on every floor to keep track of us. My colleague Richard Valeriani gathered meal chits from the rest of us and demanded caviar for breakfast.

"Nyet!"

Richard would not give up, and so finally a sizable saucer of caviar arrived and we all shared his bounty.

In the press quarters, a bar was set up with an ample supply of vodka, but since we were working it was of little use except to our Soviet minders, who we assumed were low-level Moscow cops. By noon each day they were staggering drunks, asleep at their posts or stumbling out onto the Moscow streets.

After filing reports from Moscow's central television headquarters, another dusty building with cracked windows and floors caked with dirt, we found the ride back into the city center instructive. This historic capital of the Union of Soviet Socialist Republics was bathed in a dim light to save on electrical generation. For most of the White House press corps, this was a first visit to America's great adversary. We had a common reaction: This is the great bogeyman, the symbol of Lenin's dream of a workers' paradise?

We began to get word that the Nixon-Brezhnev negotiations were not going well. Brezhnev and Nixon had reached agreement on a new trade relationship, but the president was pushing for a dramatic breakthrough on nukes. The big issue was a cap on MIRVs, the nuclear missiles with more than one warhead. They were especially difficult to defend against, and the president hoped for an agreement he could take back to the United States as an example of his grasp of the most important challenges in the nuclear age.

Brezhnev may have been fond of Nixon, but he wasn't eager to do a historic arms deal with a president who might be headed to jail. So the two retreated to Brezhnev's dacha on the Black Sea, a favorite vacation spot for Russian officials and Soviet workers in the vicinity.

We were effectively in Yalta, the Black Sea resort where Joseph Stalin met with President Roosevelt and Prime Minister Churchill near the end of World War II and created the postwar Soviet empire, including control over Poland, Czechoslovakia, Hungary, East Germany, and smaller but important East European states. American critics of the deal blamed the ailing Roosevelt for conceding far too much to Stalin, and so "Yalta" had a deeply negative standing as a place for a modern summit. Instead we were quartered nearby at Oreanda.

Whatever the name, it was not exactly Malibu.

The beaches were uneven stretches of rocks rather than sand, so lumpy that sunbathers had to lie on wooden platforms instead of towels to enjoy what passed for comfort. The tourists started claiming their territory around six A.M., and so by nine the beach was covered with the large white bodies of Soviet workers and their

wives and offspring. Latecomers were forced to stand on
an uneven levee and spread their arms to catch the sun's
rays.

While Nixon and Brezhnev were still talking and dining
together, Pat Buchanan, the president's faithful speechwriter, joined Haig's military aide, George Joulwan, for a
Black Sea cruise with a few of their hard-core KGB
counterparts. Lieutenant Colonel Joulwan had just been
promoted to colonel, so a few toasts were in order. As Pat
told me later, the celebratory drinking led to more drinking and a spirited exchange on the merits of the two
systems, Soviet and American.

By the time they returned to shore, Buchanan and
Joulwan were in a militant frame of mind, so they decided to make an assault on Brezhnev's dacha, which sat
atop a steep cliff. Not surprisingly, they didn't get far
before Brezhnev's security detail intercepted them and
summoned Al Haig. They escaped a gulag and skulked
sheepishly back to the White House staff quarters. Joulwan went on to become the commanding general of the
United States European Command and supreme allied
commander Europe in 1993.

Pat and George became good friends during our
White House days, but they never gave up much information about the backstage machinations of Watergate.
I later realized that maybe what I needed was a speed-
boat on the Potomac and a case of vodka.

While we were hanging out on the Black Sea, an
amusing minidrama was unfolding back at the Kremlin,

in Moscow. Ron Ziegler had stayed behind and decided to show some friends his accommodations in the Kremlin. Ron had the proper security clearances, but his friends did not, and the Russian KGB blew up. They threw out Ziegler's visitors and summoned Homer Luther, the über–White House advance man for the trip.

Homer recalls that he was joined by an American Secret Service agent for an urgent meeting with the senior KGB agent, who then refused to talk to Homer. Homer, laughing, told me, "The Russian said, 'I will only talk to your security agent.'" So the Soviet agent would give Homer hell through the American agent, who would then turn to Homer and repeat the dressing-down. Homer was forced to become a bystander at his own punishment. The KGB man then instructed the American agent to tell Homer to tell Ziegler that he would never be allowed in the Soviet Union again.

That anecdote is a snapshot of how the Soviets operated at every level and a small but telling indication of one of the many reasons the system could not be sustained.

We returned to Washington via Minsk and the largest display I'd ever seen of caviar at the Minsk press reception. Caviar for the White House press corps, but a major disappointment for Richard Nixon, who arrived back in the States without a new arms deal, facing a vote on impeachment on August 23 organized by the House Democratic leadership.

Back in Washington, I went to a small dinner for

John Rhodes, the House Republican leader. It was an off-the-record evening because Rhodes had been invited to a White House dinner that night and decided not to attend.

His decision to skip a presidential invitation was all I needed to know.

*The Nixon family was all smiles in pictures from the
White House residence following his decision to resign.
But it's hard not to notice President Nixon's clenched fists.*

CHAPTER 26

Nixon's poll numbers were in free fall—his approval rating in July's Gallup poll was just 24 percent.

On July 24, the blockbuster decision from the U.S. Supreme Court: it ruled unanimously that Nixon had to turn over to the House Judiciary Committee the tape recordings he had hoped to protect with executive privilege. The end was in sight.

Even so, the pervasive uncertainty that had hovered over Washington for a year did not disappear entirely. The White House team persisted in its efforts to demonstrate that the president was still on the job.

A summit on the economy was organized, with the administration's top financial teams flown to Los Angeles for a series of meetings and proclamations zeroing in on inflation. Roy Ash, the head of the Office of Management and Budget, was a taciturn recruit from the private sector, where he had earned a fortune as a hard-edged management genius. Dressed in his CEO uniform of suit and tie, with the hot lights of cameras heating up the Southern California afternoon even more, Ash, true to his reputation, remained stoic and uncomplaining as reporters went through the motions of grilling him on the economy.

Finally, Helen Thomas could stand it no longer. She said, "Mr. Ash do you think the president should resign and leave office?"

He stared at her for a moment, his expression unchanged, then turned and walked away without another word. The president's stock of defenders was running dry.

When the president returned to Washington, as we learned later in Woodward and Bernstein's *The Final Days,* it was chaos behind the scenes in the White House and within the Nixon family. A review of the June 23, 1972, tape recording laid bare the president's involvement in the cover-up. He could be heard ordering Haldeman to organize a phony scenario: the CIA would tell the FBI to back off the Watergate investigation because it involved sensitive national security issues.

When Pat Buchanan and others close to the president heard that, they knew it was game over. He must resign. But Nixon and his family members believed he could survive by personally standing up to the impeachment trial and the Senate. Eventually he realized the disclosure of the tape's contents was driving away what supporters he had left.

At the same time, Gerald Ford's team was privately scrambling to prepare for his presidency, a tricky procedure because it could not appear to be a mutiny. The vice president's advisers had quietly pulled distinguished Republicans into the capital to help. I learned that when by chance I encountered Mary Scranton crossing Pennsylvania Avenue. Her husband, former Pennsylvania governor Bill Scranton, was a widely admired GOP senior statesman. I had come to know them socially through mutual friends.

"Mary," I said, "what are you doing here?"

She paused, looked around, and then confided, "Bill has been called in to help the vice president prepare for whatever is next, but I'm not supposed to talk about it."

On NBC I was able to work that important development into the news of the day without compromising Mary. Later, she laughed and said, "Tom, I was so surprised to see you I let down my guard."

Washington shifted into another gear: preparing for the inevitable. The Nixon presidency was coming to an end. The city was abuzz with speculation and anticipation as everyone wondered how the final act would play out.

On July 31, Ehrlichman was sentenced to five years in prison for his role in the attempted Watergate cover-up. Two days later, John Dean was sentenced to one to four years. By August 4, the Harris Poll showed two-thirds of the American people believed the president should be impeached. The nation's capital was awash in rumors generated by the prospect that a president was about to be thrown out.

California senator Alan Cranston called to check on

a rumor going around: that Secretary of Defense James Schlesinger had issued a command instructing American armed forces not to automatically obey an order from the commander in chief to launch a nuclear strike. I told the senator I'd heard the same rumor but had been unable to verify it.

For his part, Schlesinger later acknowledged that he had warned that if President Nixon issued a nuclear launch order, military commanders should check with him or with Secretary of State Henry Kissinger before executing it. Schlesinger, a pipe-smoking iconoclast, was not a Nixon man, and his order struck Nixon loyalists as absurd.

The president was spending his time with his melancholy family in the White House living quarters and preparing for his farewell speech to the nation.

On August 7 I had a call from the Republican senator Robert Griffin of Michigan, who said, "Mr. Brokaw, you've been very patient with me. I want you to know Senator Goldwater, Senator Hugh Scott, and Congressman John Rhodes are headed to the White House to tell the president he cannot survive the impeachment."

Griffin earlier had agonized over what to write the president, as impeachment seemed inevitable. Finally, he had warned that if the House decided to impeach, the Senate would vote on guilt or innocence. And if the president continued to resist handing over the tapes, Griffin said, he would vote to convict.

I placed a quick call to *Nightly News* in New York, where an uptight editor said, "You've got to get a second source."

Are you kidding? This is the number two Republican in the Senate and I've developed a personal relationship with him.

Get a second source, he said.

I hung up and had an idea.

Barry Goldwater, Jr., was a congressman from California. I called his office, and when he came on the line I said, "Hey, Barry, this is really something, isn't it? Your dad coming to the White House to give the president the bad news."

Barry said, "Yeah, how about that?"

That counted as a second source!

As it turns out, the president knew his time was up. He told his visitors he would address the nation the following night.

At 1600 Pennsylvania Avenue the next day, there were two separate worlds, with no common DNA. In Lafayette Square, directly across from the White House, a younger crowd in a celebratory mood had gathered, not hostile but plainly not sorry to see the president go. Some had driven through the night from New York and other liberal bastions, veterans of the anti-Nixon movement from the angry days of Vietnam, to be in front of the White House to see if Nixon would resign.

In the downstairs working rooms of the White House, the women who staffed the press operation were typically cheerful and efficient as we all awaited the president's speech to the nation. There was an air of expectancy and, frankly, relief after the pressures of the last year.

One always ebullient White House staffer rushed to

the bulletin board with a notice "about the president" and then burst into tears.

"I'm not sure *which* president," she said.

Upstairs, Richard Nixon was still the president, and word trickled down that he was spending his time with his family: Pat, his wife of thirty-four years, who had been through so much; daughters Tricia and Julie; and their husbands, Eddie and David. The president rarely played the role of paterfamilias, but today he did, organizing family photographs, with instructions to be cheerful.

Before long it was time for him to address the nation for the last time as president. It was a defensive combination: he gave the reason for the speech, but only fleetingly, and then a review of what he had accomplished and the hopes he had for the future. Those looking for an apology might still be there in Lafayette Square.

He opened his remarks that night, as he often did, by recounting the number of Oval Office speeches he had given—this one was the thirty-seventh—without saying, "This is the last one." Instead he said, "Throughout the long and difficult period of Watergate, I have felt it was my duty to persevere, to make every possible effort to complete the term of office to which you elected me. In the past few days, however, it has become evident to me that I no longer have a strong enough political base in the Congress to justify continuing that effort."

Going on, he continued to emphasize that he was preserving the political expectations of the office, noting specifically that the support of Congress in very difficult decisions is necessary. Then came the very Nixonian line, "I have never been a quitter. To leave office before my term is completed is abhorrent to every instinct in my body." And then a familiar Nixon turn: "But as president, I must put the interests of America first."

As close as he would come to an apology, an unequivocal expression of remorse, surfaced as he went on:

"I regret deeply any injuries that may have been done in the course of the events that led to this decision. I would say only that if some of my judgments were wrong—and some *were* wrong—they were made in what I believed at the time to be the best interests of the nation."

He concluded his remarks with his hope that his time in office would mean that all of our children would "have a better chance than before of living in peace rather than dying in war."

Apart from that one fleeting reference to some wrong judgments, the president did not apologize for decisions he made that catapulted the nation into a great crisis of the presidency and trust in government. He did not look the American people in the eye and say, "I selfishly put you through a terrible ordeal that threatened the very underpinning of our way of governing—the rule of law. I am deeply sorry."

Instead, we had his self-serving comments, inadequate and deeply disappointing.

On the air from Lafayette Square that night I commented that as difficult as the president said it was for him to be a quitter, it was just as difficult for him to acknowledge any kind of wrongdoing. He said he had lost his "political base," as if this were a caucus gone awry. He had missed a historic opportunity to heal the wounds of the last year.

The peaceful transfer of power in action: Ford caused an uproar with his pardon of Nixon, but the country moved on.

CHAPTER 27

THE NEXT MORNING I handed off the NBC site for live broadcasts in Lafayette Square to my colleague John Cochran. I wanted to be in the East Room for the president's farewell to his staff, to witness in person this historic moment. We know now that the president thought he had uncharacteristically overslept that morning when he discovered that his watch had stopped, just as his presidency was about to come to a halt as well. The ever-attentive Al Haig gave the soon-to-be-ex-president a single sheet of paper, saying, "We forgot to do this. Would you sign it now?" The message was one line and historic.

"I hereby resign the Office of President of the United States."

Nixon signed the paper; the proud, complicated man was now the only American president to resign the office.

The East Room of the White House was crowded with staff members assembled to hear the personal farewell from the now former president they had served. It was a mix of melancholy and relief after almost two tense years of defiance and uncertainty.

At the back of the room, my colleague from ABC News, Tom Jarriel, arrived with a god-awful haircut, explaining that he'd been on vacation and had gone to a new barber. Just then Ron Ziegler walked in, took one look at Tom, and broke out laughing. "Jarriel," he said, "that's the worst haircut I've ever seen!" I suppose that on the worst day in the life of the man he had served so loyally, Ziegler deserved the opportunity to find some distraction.

In his speech to the gathered staff, the president was plainly emotionally bereft, staring off to the side as he invoked his mother—"a saint"—and his long journey from that small house in Yorba Linda, California. He continued his resistance to finally, candidly acknowledging his role in the scandal, saying instead, "As I pointed out last night, sure, we have done some things wrong in this administration. And the top man always takes the responsibility and I have never ducked it."

As it often did with Nixon, it came down to money. Speaking of his administration, he said, "No man or no woman ever profited at the public expense or the public till. . . . Mistakes, yes, but for personal gain, never." Then, on this darkest day of his life, he turned to his financial condition: "I only wish I were a wealthy man—at the present time, I have got to find a way to pay my taxes—and if I were, I would like to recompense you for the sacrifices all of you have made to serve in government."

In his tribute to his mother, he recalled how she cared for his two brothers dying of tuberculosis and nursed four other patients at an Arizona tuberculosis center to help pay for the treatments. "Nobody will ever write a book, probably, about my mother. . . . But she was a saint."

Then came the Nixon advice that was at once for his audience and, in his often bewildering way, self-directed:

"Never get discouraged. Never be petty.

"Always remember, others may hate you, but those who hate you don't win unless you hate them.

"And then you destroy yourself."

Given all he had left behind on tape recordings, and the testimony of aides and others about Nixon's often vengeful behavior, it is the summary line about this man's complex psyche.

Then it was time to go.

Nixon and the ever-faithful Pat were accompanied to the presidential helicopter by the incoming president, Gerald Ford, and his wife, Betty. That melancholy moment took a Nixon turn when he paused at the top of the helicopter entry, turned, and raised both arms in that triumphant pose he had used so often. Here it was a kind of caricature and not the victory salute that had served him well in the past.

Richard Moore, an affable presidential aide friendly to reporters, turned to me and said, "I think I'll go fishing." Maybe not the stuff of history, but given the circumstances, I thought it made sense.

At the NBC News headquarters in Northwest Washington, I was met by David Brinkley.

"What did you think?" he asked, referring to the president in the East Room.

What do you mean? I responded

David said, in his Brinkley style, "I thought he was going to pull out a derringer and shoot himself on television."

What?

David took me to a control room to look at the television images of the president's East Room farewell. The isolated close-ups were starkly different from my impressions in the room at the time. Nixon's emotions on the screen were raw and unsettling, as if he were speaking to an unseen audience, trying to explain how it had come to this. It was an enduring lesson in the different characteristics of a television image and an in-person view.

At work on that night's report for *NBC Nightly News*, anchored by John Chancellor, I resolved that the conclusion would be Nixon's own words. Here is the account of the day and the final paragraph, drawn from Nixon's earlier reflections on his life as a lonely child in a small house on the California coastline.

The *Nightly News* report opened with the consolidation of the past and the present:

As president, Richard Nixon has drawn crowds to the vast ellipse south of the White House before, but those were triumphs.

This was not.

These people were witnesses to the saddest day in the life of Richard Nixon.

These were his last hours as president of the United States.

Then came the melancholy scene in the East Room with his family at his side, the final walk to the helicopter accompanied by the new president, Gerald Ford, and Mrs. Ford, and then the defiant salute. For the last line I paraphrased that evocative passage from his autobiography describing his childhood in a small home forty miles inland from the Pacific Ocean in Southern California: "I listened to train whistles in the night and dreamed of far-off places."

When Citizen Nixon arrived in California he was met by a large, cheering crowd at El Toro, the Marine Air Base in Orange County, a fleeting moment reflecting his past, not his future. Accompanied by Pat, their daughter Tricia, and her husband, Edward, the now ex-president was driven to La Casa Pacifica, the oceanside estate that no longer would be eligible for the perks of being the Western White House. The security detail was sharply reduced and general maintenance was now the responsibility of the Nixon family.

Once again his friends Bebe Rebozo and Robert Abplanalp, the engineer who invented the improved aerosol spray mechanism, came to his rescue, purchasing La Casa Pacifica in a deal that gave them control of nearby oceanfront acreage and allowed the Nixon family to retain control of the historic house.

The former president's troubles went well beyond real estate, however. He resigned the presidency but he was not tried on the serious charges that would have been the foundation of his impeachment. In effect, he was a defendant-in-waiting on a series of violations of significant federal statutes.

While the nation prepared for autumn after one of the most emotionally disruptive summers in American history, the new president, Gerald R. Ford, was faced with the consequential decision of what to do with Richard Nixon.

The evidence was clear: Nixon had violated several federal laws and he was no longer protected by his favorite defense, executive privilege. Should he go to trial?

President Ford listened to his old friend Phil Buchen, a well-regarded lawyer from their hometown of Grand Rapids, Michigan, and General Haig, still in place as White House chief of staff. When Buchen was told by Leon Jaworski, the Watergate special prosecutor, that it could take as long as nine months before the ex-president could be brought to trial, the new president decided time and circumstances demanded a swift and dramatic resolution of Richard Nixon's fate.

On Sunday morning, September 8, the White House announced on short notice the president would make an announcement from the Oval Office. Meredith and I were at a Sunday brunch at the home of Rod and Carla Hills. Suddenly someone said the President was about to make an important announcement from the White House.

At 11:04 A.M., President Ford walked into the Oval Office, where a small band of journalists had been assembled, looked into the television cameras, and said, "To procrastinate, to agonize, and to wait for a more favorable turn of events that may never come . . . is a weak and potentially dangerous course for a President to follow." As for Nixon and his family, "Theirs is an American tragedy in which we have all played a part. It could go on and on and on, or someone must write the end to it. I have concluded that only I can do that, and if I can, I must."

Before the new president signed the proclamation granting the pardon, he read aloud, "Now, therefore, I, Gerald R. Ford, President of the United States, pursuant to the pardon power conferred upon me by Article II, Section 2, of the Constitution, have granted and by these presents do grant a full, free, and absolute pardon unto Richard Nixon for all offenses against the United States which he, Richard Nixon, has committed or may have committed or taken part in." It had been worked out in advance that Nixon, in California, would acknowledge his wrongdoing, which he did with his own statement, saying he could now see he "was wrong in not acting more decisively and more forthrightly in dealing with Watergate."

This unexpected Sunday morning announcement shattered the early autumn calm that had begun to settle over the nation. Networks interrupted programming to carry the details and offer analyses; talk radio was all pardon, all day and night; newspapers prepared special editions. In bars and coffee shops, on campuses and in churches, in synagogues and football stadia, Richard Nixon was back in the news.

President Ford's pardon of Nixon immediately led to speculation he had been conned by Al Haig, who remained in the White House as chief of staff, with his reputation as a cunning operator intact. For his part, the new president had his own reasons for the pardon. He knew that he faced difficult problems, with inflation still running high and cutting into every family's budget. And Vietnam was coming to a chaotic end, with the North taking over the entire country, setting off an evacuation of the South by whatever means possible. American helicopters were shoved into the sea to make room for refugees on U.S. aircraft carriers. An American contractor was forced to slug refugees attempting to board his cargo plane, which was already overloaded. South Vietnamese families went to sea in fragile sampans, hoping to be picked up by friendly ships. American troops with access to helicopters and cargo planes smuggled aboard South Vietnamese families who had been indispensable aides in and around American bases. It was an ugly end to an ugly war.

Very soon after those dramatic days, it was on to covering the administration of Gerald Ford as he toured America, in effect introducing himself as the new president. At home and abroad, America was rocked by unprecedented twin catastrophes—a president forced to resign and a war lost. In some ways, sturdy Jerry Ford was perfectly cast as a reliable symbol of America's resilience. He had friends on both sides of the congressional aisle. He was conservative but not an ideologue. My working-class father, a hard-hat Democrat, liked the news that in the morning the new president fixed his own English muffin.

Henry Kissinger stayed on as secretary of state and organized a global "meet our new president" tour so allies and enemies alike could meet this middle American and his vivacious wife, Betty, a former model and dancer. They went to South Korea, Japan, Russia, China, the Philippines, Indonesia, Finland. To Spain and an audience with Francisco Franco, who was by then a shriveled little man with one of the twentieth century's bloodiest regimes, as he had supported Nazi Germany. Franco took President Ford on a ride through the streets of Madrid in an open convertible surrounded by enormous stallions guided by tall horsemen with long lances. It was more than a show, as the horses were sheathed in blankets of silver or steel, which hid the tiny dictator on his public outing.

In Yugoslavia we continued our strongman tour with an appearance by Marshal Tito, the husky Communist who held that fractious area together during WWII. Tito was a supporter of Palestinians in the Israeli neighborhood and lectured the Americans on the importance of giving them autonomy. Tito also gave President Ford a subtle lesson in command protocol. When Ford was asked a question, he had to lean forward to reach a microphone. When Tito was asked a question, his henchmen moved the microphone to him.

Tito and Franco may have been two of the commanding dictators of the twentieth century, but they were not in the company of Mao Zedong, who was still alive when we went to China, a country still behind the bamboo curtain. Beijing was stuck in the 1920s and 1930s, with aging hotels, many more bikes than cars, horse-drawn wagons in the main squares, and air so thick with dust the White House physician warned me not to jog again when I returned with soot caking my nostrils. All the Chinese were dressed in padded blue uniforms and carried out their duties with blank expressions. When I thanked one guide he looked at me sternly and said, "I did not do this for you; I did it for my chairman, Mao Zedong."

We didn't see Mao—he had a private meeting with President Ford and Secretary Kissinger—but I did have exposure to the diminutive Deng Xiaoping, who would become China's most important leader when it began a transition to a new economy, away from Communist dogma. When the American press began to complain about no substance on the trip, just tourism, Beijing rolled out Deng for a meeting with the president. In a small room with only a simple wooden desk, Deng had a stoic expression as he awaited President Ford.

When the president arrived Deng immediately said, "I understand you had an important meeting with our leader, Chairman Mao, last night." The President missed his cue, responding instead as a kind of giddy tourist: "Yes, and Betty had a wonderful time at the ballet and Susan loved the Great Wall (although about halfway up the long walk Susan confided to me, 'I could really use a Big Mac about now')." It was clear that the setup for a serious conversation in the Deng meeting had gone off the rails.

The next day I was pool reporter for a second meeting with Deng, who this time was in a jolly mood, teasing us for writing about his tobacco habit. When the president arrived Deng said convivially, "I hope you had a good rest, Mr. President." To which President Ford replied, "Yes, and I had an excellent meeting with your chairman two nights ago."

Oh, well.

The China trip was personally memorable for a new friendship. Garry Trudeau, the Yale graduate who gave the world the satirical comic strip *Doonesbury*, was along and we quickly became friends. His perceptive sense of humor was always on call. When we were at the Great Wall he turned and asked, "I don't know, Tom. You're the Huns, sweeping out of the north, would you let this stop you?" I laughed—and then saw the exchange in one of his strips later. "Hey, I was just road testing," he explained. "When you laughed I knew it would work—I can't waste this stuff on an audience of one."

Back home we stayed in touch, and Garry met Jane Pauley at our home. That friendship born on the China Wall has endured. Now we're all grandparents—Jane and Garry, Tom and Meredith. And I still laugh at his peerless touch as a satirist.

President Ford continued to struggle with inflation, the energy crisis, and the perception he had not really earned the office. What carried him through, I believe, was his down-home style, his honesty, and his very attractive family of two rambunctious boys and his high-school-senior-daughter, Susan.

And especially his wife, Betty, who had been living the constricted life of a stay-at-home mom while her husband was on the GOP dinner circuit. Now she was

suddenly the First Lady and almost immediately was di-
agnosed with breast cancer. Her candor about her condition and willingness to speak out about the need for
women to have ready access to screening earned her
new admirers instantly, which led to television appearances and her outspoken views on a wide range of wom-
en's rights issues.

Mrs. Ford went even further, talking about a pill and
alcohol addiction that had developed while she was a
suburban wife and mother. Just as the women's con-
sciousness movement was beginning to lift off, the nation had a new champion, a First Lady who was candid
about issues that had heretofore been swept under
White House carpeting. So in many ways the Ford family introduced a new, modern era to the White House,
partisan politics aside. After the Watergate scandal
America was looking for a renewal of homegrown values
and conduct. The Ford family delivered.

For his part, President Ford was a tireless campaigner,
crisscrossing the country, preparing for the upcoming
1976 presidential election. There were strong winds
blowing out of the west: California governor Ronald
Reagan was organizing a challenge for the GOP nomina-
tion.

On September 5, 1975, President Ford was in Sacra-
mento, California, as part of a west coast campaign tour,
and he began the morning working a rope line of admirers on the state capitol grounds. I was a few feet behind
him when suddenly Secret Service agents grabbed the
president. Someone yelled, "Gun!" as another agent,
Larry Buendorf, reached out and got his hand on a

.45-caliber pistol aimed right at the president by a young woman in a long red dress.

As the agents hustled the president away, another agent handcuffed the young woman, who kept shouting, "It didn't go off!" I told my colleague Russ Ward to go with the presidential party; I wanted to follow the suspect to confirm what I was sure was true. I recognized her. She was Lynette "Squeaky" Fromme, a disciple of the notorious Charles Manson, who was serving a life sentence with other members of his cult for the brutal murders in the Los Angeles hills in 1969 of the actress Sharon Tate and four others. Fromme had not been involved in the murders, but she had kept vigil outside the courthouse where Manson was on trial.

As a lone Secret Service agent guarded the now handcuffed Squeaky, I kept yelling at her, "Aren't you Squeaky Fromme?," confident that she was but wanting to be sure. She didn't respond but kept yelling, "It didn't go off!" as the stoic Secret Service agent maintained his grip on the manacles.

Racing to catch up with the official party, I arrived just in time to hear press secretary Ron Nessen say the suspect had been identified as one Lynette Fromme, address unknown. To which I added, "As in Squeaky Fromme, a member of the Manson cult." Ron started to laugh and the other reporters looked at me, puzzled, until they all realized it was true.

In a bizarre twist, another California woman, Sara Jane Moore, also tried to assassinate President Ford seventeen days later in San Francisco as he emerged from a hotel on Union Square. Her first shot missed and the second one went astray thanks to the quick action of Oliver Sipple, a former Marine who knocked her arm down.

Moore, it turns out, had developed a bizarre anti-establishment political philosophy with no real connection to President Ford except that he was an authority figure and a convenient target. Fromme and Moore served lengthy prison sentences but were eventually paroled after thirty-four and thirty-two years, respectively.

Before the 1976 presidential election, I moved on from Washington to host the *Today* show in New York, but I maintained my role in NBC's political coverage. In New York I accepted an invitation to a Hofstra University retrospective on Watergate. Standing backstage I was suddenly embraced from behind in a bear hug and heard a familiar voice say, "You know how many times I've watched you on television and thought, 'I could have sent him to prison!'"

It was Bob Haldeman.

I laughed and said, "Bob, I've never talked about your offer, and I don't want to start now!"

He laughed as well and said, "Don't worry; your secret is safe with me."

Meanwhile, Richard Nixon was reintroducing himself as a public figure, holding private dinners for journalists, coming to NBC occasionally for discussions on global affairs, even appearing on *Meet the Press*, where he acknowledged that he'd occasionally been too hard on the press.

He restored his finances with his multimillion-dollar television deal with David Frost, in which he said of his political opponents, "I gave them a sword," still reluctant to acknowledge his personal behavior as a reason for his impeachment. In contentious exchanges with Frost, Nixon persistently refused to admit that he had committed criminal acts, describing his actions as political containment, until Frost cited Nixon's taped conversations with Haldeman and Ehrlichman on how to get the money to pay off the burglars, his conversations with John Dean on how to avoid perjury charges.

As Frost continued to bore in with factual definitions of criminal behavior, Nixon began to wither on camera, finally saying of the hush money arranged by the White House, "It's possible—it's a mistake that I didn't stop it." He conceded, "I made so many bad judgments . . . mistakes of the heart rather than the head. But let me say a man in the top job . . . he's gotta have a heart but his head must always rule his heart." That rationale may have been comforting to Nixon admirers, but placed alongside his language and attitude as caught on Oval Office recordings, it was a transparent appeal for sympathy when the facts provided an entirely different conclusion.

Once the Frost interviews were completed and Nixon was financially secure again, he began to reemerge as a public figure. Admirers financed a handsome Nixon library next to his childhood home in Yorba Linda. For the 1990 dedication of the Nixon Presidential Library, I invited my mother, a lifelong Democrat and keen student of public affairs, to come with me. When I asked if she wanted to meet Nixon, she said, "You know, I would."

She had never voted for him but they shared some

common American experiences. Their families had gone through very difficult times in the 1930s. Mother's South Dakota farm family lost everything in the Great Depression; even though she graduated from high school with honors at sixteen, the cost of college—one hundred dollars a year—had been out of the question.

Nonetheless, she was a student of American literature, history, and politics, a disciple of presidents Franklin Roosevelt and Harry Truman. Mother and my dad, nicknamed "Red" for his flaming red hair, were what I called Dirt Road Democrats, chasing construction jobs across the Midwest, where Red was in high demand for his great skills operating earth-moving equipment.

After I introduced Mother to Nixon, they quickly fell into a cordial exchange about South Dakota. Mother was aware that Pat Nixon had started life in the Black Hills of our home state, where Pat's father had been a miner in a large gold mine.

I had never seen Nixon as relaxed around a stranger as he was around my mother, and Mother was plainly enjoying the moment. As we walked away I teased, "I trust this doesn't mean you're changing your party registration." She laughed and said, "No, but I had a good time."

Back in New York, a few months before I turned fifty, NBC secretly arranged for camera crews to get reactions to my milestone birthday.

One of the crew members came to my office wide-eyed, saying, "You're not going to believe this!" Another person inserted a videotape into the TV setup across from my desk, and there on the screen was Richard Milhous Nixon, in a blue suit, an American flag in his lapel, saying into the camera, "I want to wish Tom Brokaw a happy birthday. I've always thought Tom was a man of very good judgment."

A short pause, a quick smile, and then: "He never showed better judgment than when he turned down my offer to be my press secretary!"

That was my last contact with Richard Nixon, and a welcome surprise. Finally we found something on which we could agree.

*President Nixon moved back to California for a while and
then returned to the East Coast and resumed an active life
of writing and entertaining journalists. But even now,
we're left to wonder—which of the many
Richard Nixons should we believe?*

EPILOGUE

So I come to the end of this odyssey with the same question that is asked at the entrance to his library: "Who was Richard Nixon?"

He had so many identities.

Brilliant but insecure. Physically awkward but able to manage the choreography of a very public figure for more than half a century. A global visionary with myopia about his own shortcomings.

The man and the president continue to generate strong expressions of admiration and contempt. He was neither the first occupant of the Oval Office with complex personal qualities nor the last.

There does seem to be now more praise and awareness for Nixon's creation of the Environmental Protection Agency, the War on Cancer, Title IX (which expanded women's rights), lowering the voting age to eighteen, and eliminating the draft, in addition to his diplomatic masterstroke in China and arms control treaties with the USSR in his first term. That roll call of accomplishment makes his participation, language on the tapes, and deceit in the long Watergate scandal all the more perplexing and unforgivable.

The power and responsibilities are so great and even the ordinary decisions so consequential, with constant examination by the press, as well as domestic and foreign adversaries, that all presidents leave office with some scars. How the long view of history will judge him remains unanswered, as does that provocative question: Who was Richard Nixon?

ACKNOWLEDGMENTS

The White House press corps was much smaller, mostly white and male and dominated by print representatives. There were personal ideological differences within the ranks, but at the end of the day the indisputable facts of the president's policies and behavior were the central themes.

In the course of this book I mention several of my colleagues. I want to also acknowledge those who were not singled out but nonetheless were consistently professional and personally cordial in our common pursuit of the facts in a historic drama of unparalleled consequences.

Frank Cormier and Gaylord Shaw of the Associated Press; Norm Kempster of United Press International; Aldo Beckman of the *Chicago Tribune*; Marty Schram of Long Island *Newsday*; John Herbers and Philip Shabecoff of *The New York Times*; occasional visits by R.W.

"Johnny" Apple of *The New York Times*; Rudy Abramson of the *Los Angeles Times*; Larry O'Rourke of *The Philadelphia Bulletin*; Marty Nolan of *The Boston Globe*; Jim Deakin of the *St. Louis Post-Dispatch*.

There were other occasional visitors, but this was the core group not mentioned in my text.

This is my eighth book with Kate Medina, the legendary Random House editor in the corner office. Our relationship long ago became one of not just writer-editor but of family, as we worked together on *The Greatest Generation*, and books about my formative years in South Dakota, the unexpected personal encounter with cancer, and four other subjects relevant to our time.

Kate and her colleague Jon Meacham wisely thought that now is the time to revisit the final year of President Nixon through my experience as a White House correspondent. Though I was at first reluctant, I warmed to the subject as Kate and Jon persuaded me that the current political climate is a reminder that history provides context for large issues and small. So, Kate, here we go again.

As always I am dependent on a strong, perceptive assist from research experts, and no one is better than Ruby Shamir, a student of modern American politics who has written widely on the subject. She brought to Watergate and Richard Nixon a historian's discipline and a generational curiosity about the man and the time. I unfailingly welcomed her scholarship.

Once again I relied on my friend Frank Gannon for insights on the man and the time of the fall of Richard Nixon. His brilliant work on the Nixon Library, especially the provocative essay greeting visitors—"You Decide: Who Was Richard Nixon ?"—was a perfect ignition for where I hoped to go.

I am grateful to the entire team at Random House, including Kate's right hand, Erica Gonzalez, who helped shepherd this project and wrangle all of its pieces into a coherent whole. I'm grateful for the assistance of Louisa McCullough. Thanks to the leadership of Random House for giving my books a place in their library: Gina Centrello, president and publisher of Random House; Bill Takes, executive vice president; and Avideh Bashirrad, vice president and deputy publisher. Thanks to Evan Camfield for his copyediting genius; Carole Lowenstein, who has done the interior design of all of my Random House books; Benjamin Dreyer, coordinator extraordinaire, who also has brought his expertise to all of my Random House books; Greg Kubie, my publicist for the book; Ayelet Gruenspecht, the marketer on the book; and Anna Bauer, Joe Perez, and Paolo Pepe who did the cover design.

Finally, a big shout out to the home team led by Meredith and including our family business manager, Geri Jansen; house manager, Goldine Nicholas; and my NBC executive assistant, Mary Casalino.

PHOTO CREDITS

The White House Photo Office Collection/Byron Schumacher/WHPO-E1729-02A

66 Bettmann/Getty Images

80 AFP Files/AFP/Getty Images

84 Keystone Press/Alamy Stock Photo

88 AP Images

94 Everett Collection Historical/Alamy Stock Photo

98 H. Armstrong Roberts/ClassicStock/Alamy Stock Photo

104 AP Images/John Rous

110 AP Images

120–21 Dirck Halstead/The LIFE Images Collection/Getty Images

122 AP Images

128 AP Images

134 The Richard Nixon Presidential Library and Museum/ The White House Photo Office Collection/Jack Kightlinger/WHPO-9512-03A

140 AP Images/Michel Lipchitz

146 AP Images

150 AP Images

154 The Richard Nixon Presidential Library and Museum/ The White House Photo Office Collection/Jack Kightlinger/WHPO-E2678-14

158 AP Images

162 Bettmann/Getty Images

166 The Richard Nixon Presidential Library and Museum/ The White House Photo Office Collection/Oliver Atkins/WHPO-E2938-22

170 AP Images

180 The Richard Nixon Presidential Library and Museum/ The White House Photo Office Collection/Oliver Atkins/WHPO-E3359-05A

188 David Hume Kennerly/Getty Images

206 CORBIS/Corbis/Getty Images

BACK ENDPAPER: Bettman/Getty Images

INDEX

Page numbers in *italics* indicate photographs.

ABOUT THE AUTHOR

Tom Brokaw is the author of seven bestsellers: *The Greatest Generation*, *The Greatest Generation Speaks*, *An Album of Memories*, *A Long Way from Home*, *Boom!*, *The Time of Our Lives*, and *A Lucky Life Interrupted*. A native of South Dakota, he graduated from the University of South Dakota with a degree in political science. He began his journalism career in Omaha and Atlanta before joining NBC News in 1966. Brokaw was the White House correspondent for NBC News during Watergate, and from 1976 to 1981 he anchored *Today* on NBC. He was the sole anchor and managing editor of *NBC Nightly News with Tom Brokaw* from 1983 to 2005. In 2008 he anchored *Meet the Press* for nine months following the death of his friend Tim Russert. He continues to report for NBC News, producing long-form documentaries and providing expertise during breaking news events. Brokaw has won every major award in broadcast journalism, including two duPonts, two Peabody Awards, and several Emmys. In 2014, he was awarded the Presidential Medal of Freedom and he is the recipient of the French Legion of Honor. He lives in New York and Montana.

ABOUT THE TYPE

This book was set in Fairfield, the first typeface from the hand of the distinguished American artist and engraver Rudolph Ruzicka (1883–1978). Ruzicka was born in Bohemia (in the present-day Czech Republic) and came to America in 1894. He set up his own shop, devoted to wood engraving and printing, in New York in 1913 after a varied career working as a wood engraver, in photoengraving and banknote printing plants, and as an art director and freelance artist. He designed and illustrated many books, and was the creator of a considerable list of individual prints—wood engravings, line engravings on copper, and aquatints.